MOTORCYCLE ADVE

Beyond Bucharest

BOB GODDARD

Timbuktu Publishing

Published by **Timbuktu Publishing**
Stables Bungalow, Mill Reach, Buxton, Norwich, NR10 5EJ
www.timbuktu-publishing.co.uk

ISBN 978-0-9563518-0-7

British Library Cataloguing in Publication Data available.

Design and layout by Esther Lemmens
www.estherlemmens.co.uk

Printed by Cromwell Press Group

*With special thanks to Esther Lemmens, Turton Middleton Ltd
and Nick Cordell.*

Cover image: Veliko Tarnovo, Bulgaria
© Bogdan Postelnicu

For EveryChild's children
May they live their dreams

Royalties from the sale of this book
will be donated to EveryChild

If you'd like to know more about sponsoring a child or making a
donation, go to: ***www.everychild.org.uk*** *or contact them at*
EveryChild, 4 Bath Place, Rivington Street, London EC2A 3DR.
Telephone 020 7749 2468.

Contents

Introduction

THAT Ewan McGregor had a lot to answer for. I leafed again through page after page of my AA Glovebox Atlas Europe and felt a rising tide of panic. This was all Ewan's fault.

His twinkling eyes and cheeky smile had captivated my wife Viv as we followed on TV his 'Long Way Round' motorbike marathon with his biking buddy Charley Boorman. Very soon pictures of Ewan, carefully snipped out of the Radio Times, started appearing pinned to notice boards and office calendars.

He was charming, rugged and handsome. And he was smiling down at me from astride his BMW GS1150 while I ate my breakfast. It was time to get out of my dressing gown and into my bike leathers before it was too late and Viv had completely re-wallpapered the bungalow with little scrapbook Ewans. I'd have to take her on a two-wheeled adventure of our own.

This had started off as a casual suggestion to cheer her up as she lamented the end of the TV series. But it rapidly got out of hand. Impressed with Ewan and Charley's visits to Unicef charity operations in Ukraine, Kazakhstan and Mongolia, Viv suggested we could do something similar for UK charity EveryChild, which had allowed us to visit its project in Malawi the previous year.

This had been a real eye-opener. We'd been blown away by the quality of EveryChild's work and by the astonishing amount they achieved, with very little money, to improve the lives of children and their families. As a result we'd ended up helping to fund the building of a new school block and the drilling of wells in the village of the little girl we sponsored there. Now that we were sponsoring another child in Bulgaria, well, perhaps we should hop on our motorbikes and head there?

The next step was a visit to EveryChild's London HQ. Yes, they'd be delighted if we helped raise the profile of their projects in Bulgaria... and how about Romania, Moldova and the Ukraine?

Mmm. This was beginning to sound like a fairly epic bike ride, even though the last two countries were ruled out when we discovered we couldn't extend our bike insurance that far. As I traced my finger along our likely route, and followed the maps through country after country, it finally dawned on me what I'd foolishly talked myself into: a motorcycle expedition to the Black Sea and, fingers crossed, back home again.

It might not be 'Around The World in 80 Filming Opportunities' like Ewan and Charley, but it was quite enough for a pair of dithery grandparents who found London pretty scary. Just the trip to EveryChild's office in the British capital left us confused and bewildered. The crowds, the traffic, the tube trains all filled us with that slightly breathless feeling that precedes a panic attack. Were we really cut out for the mad speeds of the German autobahns? Could we cope with the chaos of Bucharest? Would we survive the potholes of Poland and the barmy drivers of Bulgaria? Only time would tell...

We certainly had the bikes for the job. Viv's 650cc Honda Transalp and my 1000cc Honda Varadero were built for long distance touring, even if we weren't. They were a pair of V-twin machines with luggage to match, just crying out for a chance to stretch their legs. We'd always joked that the Transalp wouldn't be happy until it had lived up to its name, so maybe we could ride over the Alps on the way?

Hang on a minute... this meant passing through France, Germany, Austria, Slovenia, Croatia, Hungary, Romania and Bulgaria on the way out, and if we fancied a change of scenery with a more northerly route, Bulgaria, Romania, Hungary, Slovakia, Poland, Germany, the Netherlands, Belgium and France on the way back. Twelve countries and sixteen border crossings. Blimey!

I'd obviously been suffering from a senior moment. What had I been thinking of when I agreed to this? These days a 100-mile journey wears me out and this looked like a 5,000-mile round trip. I don't like driving at night any more, arthritic thumb joints make long distance biking painful and I need a nap after lunch most days. Ah, the joys of growing older.

Viv was no spring chicken either. After decades as a pillion passenger, she'd finally plucked up the courage to take her motorcycle test six years previously. Since then she'd picked up a permanent knee injury from a crash in New Zealand and was left with a weak back after trying to lift a fallen bike. Would she have the strength to wrestle her tall and heavily loaded Transalp through the traffic and torn-up roads of Eastern Europe? Did either of us old codgers have the stamina to see this through?

Unlike Ewan and Charley, we wouldn't have a fleet of support vehicles to provide fixers, doctors, creature comforts and peace of mind. We would be on our own if anything went wrong. We were clearly out of our tiny minds.

Too late to back out now. EveryChild had made arrangements with their project leaders in Romania and Bulgaria. The media had been primed to expect our arrival. We'd reassured our understandably worried grown-up kids we'd be fine. And we'd arranged for our neighbour to look after the cats. There were too many people to let down. We *had* to go.

The bikes were serviced, tyres replaced, spare bulbs taped under seats, GB stickers stuck on. Finally our panniers and topbox were stuffed with clothes plus extra underwear in case of emergencies, leaving just enough room for a travel kettle and a miniature CD player. As long as we had a cup of tea and Bob Dylan to soothe us, we figured we could face whatever the road ahead had in store.

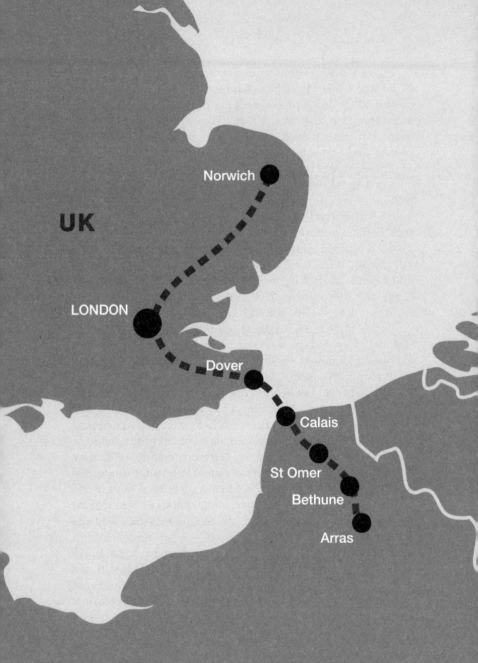

Norwich

UK

LONDON

Dover

Calais

St Omer

Bethune

Arras

FRANCE

1

It Ain't Half Hot Mum!

Day 1, Thursday June 23rd, Norfolk

Suddenly it was D-Day and, in a searing heatwave, we were stumbling around like Laurel and Hardy. Neither of us wanted to put on our helmets and jackets, but we couldn't ride without them. It was late June and Europe was broiling in a spell of fiercely hot and humid weather which had us dripping as we wobbled out on to the back lanes of Norfolk at 8am.

By the time we'd battled through the Norwich rush hour, then stopped to fill the bikes' tanks, we were sweltering. As the sun rose higher, the temperature soared with it and even with the slipstream at motorway speeds I could feel the steady trickle of perspiration making its way down to my nether regions.

Ladies don't perspire, of course, but when we took a break at Thurrock Services on the M25, Viv was all aglow with red face and matted hair. She headed off to the washrooms to freshen up and was gone such a long time I was beginning to wonder if she'd had another Egyptian bathroom moment. Once, when visiting a brand new public loo in Luxor, the entire cubicle door came away in her hand and wedged itself at 45 degrees, blocking the passageway. Someone had forgotten to fit the hinges, which was a tad inconvenient. Ah, the joys of foreign travel.

Luckily no toilet dramas this time. Viv was splashing her face with water and so enjoying the cool of the subterranean loos, she was reluctant to resurface into the fierce heat of the day.

Despite our cooling down stop we pitched up at the Eurotunnel at noon, two hours early for our train. By now it was blisteringly hot, the tarmac was melting and so were we as the traffic marshal made us wait with our ticking, heat-shimmering bikes under the midday sun. Two hours of this and we'd expire from heat exhaustion. No problem, said the Eurotunnel man, we could board the 12.33 train – yippee!

By now there was a group of us bikers, all shedding layers and looking frazzled. Several were heading for motorcycle racing at the Assen circuit in The Netherlands, and a BMW-mounted couple were riding to Klosters in Switzerland. I deliberately held back in order to follow the others up the ramp and into the side-door of the carriage. This is tricky with a fully loaded touring bike, especially when you are short of leg and weak of limb, and I didn't want to drop it right in front of them. Instead we copied them wobbling down the channels designed for car wheels and finally came to rest on our side-stands as buzzers sounded, doors closed and… nothing seemed to happen. Then we realised the train had silently started to creep forward, gathering pace as it slipped beneath the English Channel.

While I thought about the millions of tons of water above our heads, Viv looked relaxed and happy. She hates any kind of boat travel, so we'd given the cross-channel ferry the heave-ho in favour of the tunnel option. It was a good choice. Thirty smooth and effortless minutes later, we emerged into a new country and a new time zone, where it was, if anything, even hotter.

First stop was a fuel station where we filled up the bikes with *sans plomb* and ourselves with *jambon fromage baguettes*. France was cooking in the 30°-plus heat wave and, unbeknown to us, thousands of elderly folk were dying of heat-stroke in Paris. We had cleverly picked the hottest moment in recorded history to ride through northern France. Despite standing in the shade to munch our lunch, sweat dripped steadily off our chins and elbows and neither of us fancied getting back on our hot machines.

Risking imminent meltdown, we reluctantly pulled our helmets, jackets and gloves back on and continued on the soft and bubbling tarmac. Despite confusing signs we eventually found ourselves on the right road for St Omer heading south east into flat French countryside, between rows of poplars. Perhaps foolishly, considering the distance we planned to cover, we'd decided to avoid motorways wherever possible and take the more interesting, scenic route. The downside of this plan soon became apparent. Chugging through countless villages and small towns, our progress was agonisingly slow and without the speed of the open road, there was no breeze to cool us and we sweltered. By the time we rolled into the stop-start traffic of Bethune, we were desperate for relief from the oppressive heat. We needed to find some shade and get out of our oven-like jackets and brain-boiling helmets. Stuck in a queue for distant traffic lights our bikes became unbearable two-wheeled radiators, so we pulled over for a kerbside pitstop in the shade of a three-storey building, tore off most of our clothes and slumped, panting, to the pavement. Fortunately the locals were too hot to take any notice of this unseemly behaviour. We drank two bottles of water and steamed.

Both our Hondas are blessed with efficient fairings and tall screens, excellent at deflecting wind and rain in cold weather, but in a heatwave like this they trap the heat of the engines in an unwelcome bubble of hot air around the rider. As we remounted, all we could do was open our jackets and helmet visors to let some air circulate and, in my case, remove my gloves to cool my sweaty palms and let a draught up my sleeves.

If we'd been hoping for a Ewan McGregor *"I'm so in love with my bike!"* moment, this wasn't it. I'd have swapped mine right then for a Lada with air conditioning. With jackets flapping and steam issuing from every orifice, we rode into Arras where we planned to stay for the night – and promptly got lost. This did nothing to help to cool us down, either physically or mentally, so we probably didn't appreciate the fine architecture of the towering spire of Le Beffroi and l'Hotel de Ville or the distinctive Dutch gables overlooking la Place des Héros, quite as much as we should have done.

Despite massive destruction during three First World War battles (the Somme is nearby), Arras is today a town of great beauty and rich history. But it was lost on us as we struggled through the late afternoon heat to find Rue Cambrai. Finally, frazzled and weary, sodden with sweat and sticky with insects, our first day's ride came to an end as we stumbled across Hotel Balladins.

I'd booked this, the only pre-planned accommodation of the trip, online the day before and was pleased I had.

"Oui, Monsieur Godarrrr, we 'ave a rum for you," was music to my ears. We love France and the French, but they can be sniffy about letting bikers into their hotels. Some years earlier, on a two-up trip to La Rochelle on the Varadero, we were turned away from several small hotels in northern France. On two occasions a hanging sign in the window was turned from *'Chambres'* to *'Complet'* when we rolled up and started to clamber off the bike. In another hotel the manager watched me waddle across his lobby in a rustle of waterproof nylon overtrousers, and didn't even glance at his board full of dangling room keys before he announced:

"M'sieur, zee 'otel is full."

I would almost prefer the truth...

"Non! We don't want dirty, smelly motorcyclists in our nice, clean 'otel, So peess off!"

On that occasion, we'd finally given up and sought the help of a tourist information office, where a helpful lady phoned a nearby hotel for us, got confirmation that they had a room vacant for an English couple. And – when I insisted she asked – available for an English couple *'avec un moto'*.

Now at the Balladins, the relief we felt when he confirmed our booking was overwhelming. I don't think we could have ridden any further in that heat. We'd done just 258 miles since leaving home that morning and were like a pair of wrung-out dishcloths. How on earth we were going to get all the way to Bulgaria, I could not imagine. Oh well, one day at a time.

We lugged our bags (so that's why it's called luggage!) to a pokey little room full of stale, hot air. But we didn't care because it had a shower where we could wash away the grime and sweat and some of the aches and pains of our first day on the road. Refreshed, we set to tackling our unsavoury laundry. Sweaty T-shirts, socks and underwear were washed and hung out of the window to dry.

We didn't have the luxury of a balcony for drying clothes, but we were delighted to find that among the mod cons was a television set boasting an information option. Viv spotted the remote control featured an 'info' button, and pressed it.

The TV promptly responded with *'pas de info'* – *no information* – which said it all.

Finally, feeling semi-human again, we went down to the restaurant for dinner and a chance to unwind. But first we had to decipher the menu, which had fancy-smancy names for each of the dishes and was made no clearer when the Chinese waitress volunteered a 10-minute explanation of every item's ingredients and preparation in – as far as we could tell – Cantonese!

Between us, Viv and I cope fairly well with French. I was kicked out of French class at the age of 12 due to woeful incompetence and persistent sniggering at the French word for swimming pool, *la piscine*, on the grounds that Mr Lumley, our PE teacher, had told us we shouldn't. Viv, on the other hand, was a model student and made it all the way to French A level but failed her exams when a young tyke on a bike – a Honda 90 – distracted her from her studies. That tyke was me, and I like to think I was worth more than a certificate that would by now be old, faded and dog eared. Hang on, that sounds horribly like me after all!

I usually launch into an enthusiastic Franglais of the Del-Boy variety and am rescued by Viv's more scholarly linguistics. But on this occasion both our brains had been so thoroughly *sautéed* inside our helmets, all either of us could think of was *'mange tout, mange tout'* followed by fits of giggles. So we were lucky we got anything at all.

We eventually became so desperate for something to eat we just nodded vigorously when our waitress approached with her pad, and pointed at menu entries which we fervently hoped were not snails or frogs' legs. I received something that looked like lamb and pasta, while Viv's fish dish was described on the dish-of-the-day board as *'filet de haddcok'* which set her off giggling again.

It was good to see her laugh, as today could have been both the start and end of our trip. A couple of days previously, Viv had panicked big time. In floods of tears, she had admitted that she was scared. Scared of riding her bike on the continent. Scared of suffering unendurable backache or knee ache. Scared of getting so far and then being unable to go any further.

"Look," I'd said, in my best soothing voice, *"you can ride down to Kent, can't you?"*

"Yes," she sniffled into a screwed-up tissue.

"And the train ride through the tunnel will be a doddle, a chance to relax and unwind. And if you find you can't cope with riding in France, we'll simply turn around and come back. Okay?"

"Okay."

"We'll take it one day at a time, and if at any point either of us finds it's too much, we'll give up and come back. Is that a deal?"

"Okay. Thanks. Sorry I'm so pathetic."

In fact, Viv's back and knees had been sore and painful for the first couple of hours on French roads today. But once we realised it was due to stress and holding herself as stiff as a statue, things got better, if not my jokes…

"You're just too tense – almost a marquee!" I told her. *"Remember the old bottom-yoga you invented in New Zealand? You need some knee and back yoga now."*

I was referring to a technique Viv had devised while we were riding little traillie bikes with rock-hard seats a few years before*. This routine for flexing and exercising while riding along proved essential for long spells in the saddle, and adapting it for this new situation soon loosened up Viv's lactic-locked muscles and got her joints moving again.

"I'm okay, by the way," she said, as she squeezed my hand among the dinner plates and gazed romantically into my eyes that first evening.

"I'm ready for another day of French motorcycling – I think I can do it," she smiled. It looked like there'd be a Day Two after all.

We stumbled out of the restaurant, replete with haddcok, and bumped into two more British bikers who were staying in Arras on a war graves research mission. One had raced in the Isle of Man TT, the other rode a BMW GS1150, like half the population of the UK, it seems, following Ewan and Charley's 'Long Way Round' exploits on the same machines.

After swapping tales of derring-do for half an hour, we made our excuses and walked into town. This was partly for the exercise before bedtime (Ah, the joys of growing old), partly to buy reasonably priced water after being charged an arm and a leg for two small bottles of the stuff when we arrived, and partly to see if I recognised any of the streets, hotels or restaurants.

Described in 'Land Of The Long Wild Road', the book of our antipodean exploits on two wheels (see end of this chapter for details)

Arras had been my first-ever overnight stop on foreign soil way back in 1976, and it had been a memorable event. I was just 23, the newly-appointed features editor of Motorcycle Mechanics magazine. Within weeks of joining this illustrious journal, I was summoned to the editor's house where he was lying flat on his back with a slipped disc.

"You're off to cover the Milan motorbike show," announced Colin Mayo. *"I can't go – obviously – so you will take my place in the car with Peter, the advertising manager. I hope your passport is up to date."*

I didn't like to admit I'd never had a passport, or that this supposedly well-travelled features editor had never been outside the UK and was quaking at the prospect. Two weeks later, clutching my brand new passport and an old French school book that I thought might come in handy if I needed more than a swimming pool, we drove off the Dover-Calais ferry and into a land of wonder and delight.

Seems daft now, but I remember being gobsmacked at how *French* everything was. The houses, the streets, the road signs, the shops, the people... everything was so completely different from the UK. I was wide-eyed and open-mouthed, which wasn't too clever as I was driving at the time.

Peter and his two pals, who were coming along for the ride, told me that they were fully experienced in international travel and knew how to get along famously in France. And the quickest way for me to learn was to drive the first stint, straight off the ferry.

When we pulled up outside a little hotel in Arras, I was despatched to go find us a cheap room for the four of us. *"It'll do you good... help you get to grips with the lingo... nothing to it."* Peter assured me. Being the innocent abroad, I didn't question this and went to find the hotel owner.

It wasn't until the following day, when I witnessed Peter speaking English very loudly and waving his arms around a lot, that I realised my travelling companions had even less command of French than I did. A few miles after shouting instructions in pidgin English at a petrol pump attendant, Peter realised the Frenchman had fleeced him out of a hundred Francs.

My first go at speaking French to the hotel owner was more successful.

"Avez vous une chambre avec quatre lits, s'il vous plait?"

I was pleased to remember a few words from my misspent schooldays, and even more delighted when *madame* understood my atrocious pronunciation and showed me a big, high-ceilinged room containing four beds, at a stunningly low price.

I was so thrilled with my mastery of the language and so taken with all things French, that I rather overdid it that evening while celebrating my first day on French soil. At the nearby restaurant, a fixed-price meal came with four choices of starter, so naturally we ordered a different one each and shared them: onion soup, pâté and toast, marinated mussels and mixed salad were washed down with a couple of bottles of the local red wine. This was followed by chicken and chips and another bottle of wine, followed by apple tart and a brandy apiece.

Positively glowing by now, we staggered a few yards to a little late-night bar called, improbably, 'Chez Lulu' and decided it would be a noble sign of solidarity with our new-found French *amis* if we drank the same tipple as them. The drinks looked innocuous enough… rather like glasses of milk.

The only thing you can do with a half-pint glass of aniseed liqueur and water, when you realise you've made a terrible mistake but don't want to look like a complete wuss, is to swallow it. I vaguely remember trying to show the bemused local lads how to play pool, only to discover that their table didn't have any pockets, which seemed very strange, and then the room started to spin.

I will draw a veil over the rest of my stay in Arras that first night, except to say that we beat a hasty retreat next morning and I wasn't in any fit state to drive for the next 24 hours.

Fortunately, as a much more sober and responsible traveller of late middle age, none of the citizens of Arras recognised me, and I couldn't identify the hotel, restaurant or even 'Chez Lulu'. We did, however, find a little greengrocer's shop still open and selling water at a more easily-swallowed price than at our hotel. Clutching two large bottles, we tottered wearily back under a surreal pink sky to our stale and pokey little room and crashed out.

Land Of The Long Wild Road was our first book of motorcycle adventures, following three months and 11,000 kilometres on two small trail bikes, riding the old gold miners' trails and sheep drovers' routes through the beautiful wilderness of New Zealand. You can still buy a copy: see the back of this book for full details

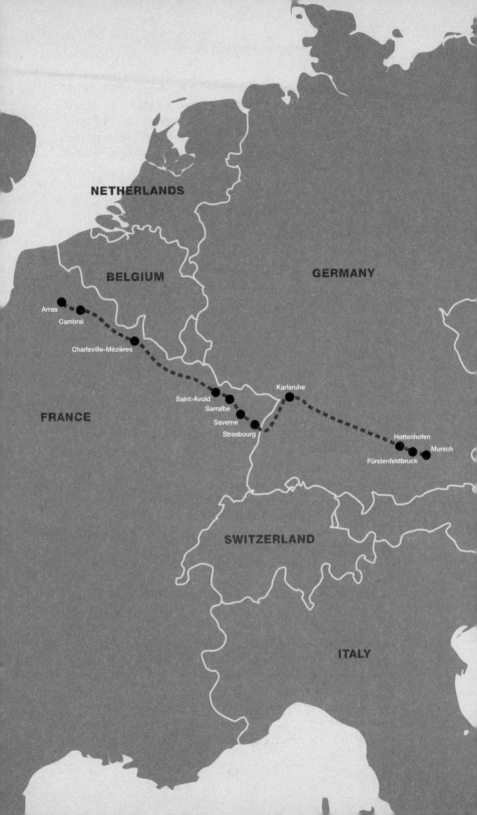

2

Chain Reactions

Day 2, Friday June 24th, Arras

Breakfast was not included in our room price, so we devoured the fruit we'd bought the night before, with tea and coffee courtesy of our trusty mini-kettle, before I set to cleaning a million dead bugs off the bikes while Viv packed the bags.

On our way out, Christophe, the owner-manager, asked if we'd had breakfast and when I replied 'Non', he deducted the price from the bill. We were 300 miles away when we discovered he'd taken off the price of our evening meals by mistake, so our first night in France proved to be relatively inexpensive.

The day was already humid and heavy with heat as we got back on the road and headed for Cambrai through lots of villages and small towns and frustratingly slow moving traffic. By the time we crossed the river Meuse at Charlesville-Méziers it was time for a coffee break and right on cue we spotted a roadside café signalled by a motorbike perched on a pole. It served as a magnet for bikers, and while the owner was chatting up Viv, telling her of his past exploits on two wheels, more motorcycles pulled up.

These were British bikers of the superbike persuasion, all fancy one-piece racing leathers and knee sliders, on their way back from a blast across Germany, where we were headed next. They told us scary stories of high-speed motorists overtaking them unexpectedly on the autobahns, and told us to watch out for loony drivers, which did nothing for Viv's confidence.

15

It was another baking hot day and we were sticky and steaming by the time we pulled into Longuyon, close by the Belgium and Luxembourg borders, for lunch. We rode into the town square which was being dressed up with banners and bunting for a festival and found a very welcoming café. The manageress invited us to eat the baguettes we'd bought at a shop down the street, while sitting at her shady outdoor table where we could keep an eye on our bikes and luggage. She even phoned to book a hotel in St Avold for us that night, which won her the top-café-lady-of-the-trip-so-far award.

We pressed on past a town called Herney *("...they won't forget Herney!")*, through an impossibly hot afternoon and stopped in Metz to cool off. It was rush hour and a repeat of the previous day's combination of traffic, temperature and tiredness. Mercifully, just as we reached the point of heat exhaustion, some riverside trees appeared and we slumped bonelessly to the ground beneath them, two panting puddles of perspiration. The temperature was now in the high thirties with intense humidity and not a breath of wind. We lay there for an hour, gasping and re-hydrating with 2 litres of water, until the traffic had started to thin and our bikes had cooled sufficiently to get back on them again.

When we got under way there was barely time to make our 7pm check-in deadline at the Hotel Campanile on Avenue du Géneral Patton in St Avold. We'd ridden out of the World War One trenches and into World War Two tank-battle hill country on the German border near Saarbrucken. We passed a cemetery for Patton's fallen troops and a huge commemorative fountain in the centre of a roundabout on the way into town. Then we spotted the hotel and its last-minute guests, like us, rushing to reception before our reservations were cancelled. It was far too hot to be searching for alternative accommodation.

The Campanile was modern and comfortable, but had rooms arranged on three floors of a separate block, accessible via external stairwells and walkways, which was a little unusual. We were too tired and sweaty to take much notice, except to grumble at having to drag our heavy bags and riding gear up to the top floor.

Two hefty panniers unclipped from frames on the Varadero's flanks and a capacious topbox from the back of the Transalp. In addition we had a rucksack containing our overtrousers, camera, map, bottles of water and snacks – things we needed to hand en-route. Plus of course, we had two full face crash helmets, two pairs of gloves and two heavy motorcycling jackets to lug upstairs too. It was too much to carry on one trip, so we had to clump wearily up and down the stairs twice before we could finally peel off our dripping clothing and cool down in the shower.

Then it was back down to the reception/restaurant block to grab a meal before the restaurant shut. We shared an outside table with two middle-aged French couples who were on their way to their German holiday homes. It's not only the Brits who have been bitten by the foreign property bug.

After supper we walked back up the hill to the impressive fountain, figuring the falling water would help to cool us down. But as the day's light faded to a peach haze, the first rumbles of thunder boomed across the sky and we hurried back to our room to get out of our unbearable clothes once again.

The heavy, clammy, pre-storm weather had unfortunate consequences. With the front window and door left slightly ajar – they were the room's only ventilation – Viv was standing naked in front of the TV, searching for a weather channel, when she looked round to see a chap staring in the door at her. Too hot and weary to care, Viv turned back to the TV and he shuffled off. Viv's not normally so casual about flashing her bits.

"Well, it was too hot to make a fuss and I decided I'd never see him again, so what if he copped an eyeful," she said.

She gave up on the TV when the weather made its intentions clear outside. Jagged streaks of lightning crackled across the sky and the cracks and kerrumps of thunder shook the building. A minute later there was a muffled shriek from the bathroom where Viv had attempted to flush the loo (white button) and inadvertently switched on the automatic wall heater (white button) instead. This gave seven minutes of pre-programmed intense heat – there was no off switch – and turned the bathroom into a sauna. Just what we needed.

Finally the much-heralded rain fell in sheets and the temperature dropped a few degrees as we tried to sleep through the noisiest, flashiest night we could remember.

Chapter 2

Day 3, Saturday June 25th, St Avold

We woke to a rain-washed dawn and set off for Strasbourg and the German border with a new plan. After the painfully slow and stickily hot progress of the past two days, we would ride the motorways to Munich. This was not without considerable apprehension from Viv, who was thoroughly rattled by the superbike riders' tales of autobahn madness.

Before we could try out the Teutonic tarmac, however, we had to ride two short sections of French toll-autoroute, which caused confusion. At the first *péage*, the toll-collector girl let me pay for both bikes and waved me through, only to lower the barrier again before Viv had a chance to get going. With no sign of it going up again and Viv stuck at the front of the queue, I parked my bike and walked back. But the girl couldn't explain what the problem was in words that made any sense to us and having paid for two bikes, I wasn't about to pay again.

The standoff was resolved when the waiting car drivers lost their cool and started shouting at her, waving their arms and sounding their horns. She raised the barrier and Viv rode through. Strange…

After the next *péage*, where I insisted Viv lined up alongside me at the barrier and we made a speedway style start together, we stopped for a giggle and a drink of water in a lay-by. It was here that I noticed, to my horror, that my bike's drive chain was as tight and rigid as an iron bar.

I was mortified by this discovery as my bike had gone for six years and 16,000 miles without ever showing signs of chain troubles. I had diligently kept it clean and lubricated and adjusted to the factory's recommended 40mm of free play. I had never had reason to doubt its reliability… until, that is, the bikes were serviced a week before we set off.

I'd given explicit instructions that the chains on both bikes were not to be touched by the mechanics. There were two reasons for this: 1) I use a special type of chain lube that dries on the chains and does not fling off to coat the back of the bike in filthy grease, unlike the stuff the bike shops use, and 2) I didn't trust the mechanics to get the chain tension correct, as few understand the need for extra slack in the chains on bikes with long-travel suspension, like our two adventure-trail machines.

So I was understandably miffed when we went to pick up the bikes, only to find both bikes' chains slathered up with horrible black grease, and my Varadero's chain tightened to 25mm free play – almost half that recommended by Honda. I was livid and had a stand-up row outside the showroom with the shop's owner.

Only after I'd produced the bike's handbook and he'd measured the chain's free play himself, did he finally agree that my chain had been incorrectly adjusted. We wheeled my Honda back into the workshop where his chief mechanic said that the chain was fine as it was and he was going home! What he was really saying was, he wasn't having some know-nothing bike owner tell him – a trained mechanic – how to adjust a motorbike chain correctly.

Eventually he thought better of his hard-line stand and returned with a spanner, saying: *"If you want your chain slack, you can have it as bloody slack as you want!"* And he proceeded to set the chain at the correct 40mm, with much muttering under his breath, before throwing the spanner on the floor and marching off in high dudgeon.

Finally the shop owner apologised for the mistake and for his chief mechanic's behaviour, and knocked a little bit off the bill, but I was still seething over the incident days later when we set off on our big trip. And that, I thought, was almost certainly why I was having this problem now, in a lay-by on the French-German border.

Horrified that my chain had suddenly gone tight, I now removed the bike's panniers and seat in order to get at the toolkit. Then I straightened and pulled out the split pin before undoing the rear axle locknut, and then slackened the adjuster nuts and bolts on the swingarm. Still no slack. I undid the adjusters some more. Still no slack! My God, what's going on?

Then I noticed the top run of the chain – until now hidden behind the chainguard – was hanging down on the swingarm with buckets of slack in it, while the lower run was still bar-taut. And finally it dawned on me… the chain appeared tight because I'd left the bike in gear to stop it rolling forward on the gentle slope where we'd parked. The in-gear engine was braking the rear wheel, by stretching the lower run of the chain tight!

Doh! There had never been a chain tension issue after all!

With the service aggro still fresh in my mind, I'd imagined a problem that didn't exist. I'd jumped to false conclusions and switched my brain into neutral instead of checking to find the cause. What a dipstick!

It took another 20 minutes to get the chain correctly reset, the tools packed away, the chain-lube cleaned off my hands, and the seat and panniers re-fitted. And much longer for my red-faced embarrassment to fade. I'd just spent an hour struggling under the blistering sun to correct a non-existent problem. What a prize prat! In fact, since we were still in France, a Noilly Prat!

Viv, meanwhile, was saying nothing. She was thinking about the dreaded German autobahns and near-misses with 200mph Mercedes, as described by those loony Brit-bikers. We kitted up and set off, both of us quiet for different reasons, to cross the Rhine.

My mood lightened as we passed Karlsruhe and I realised that for the past few miles I'd been unconsciously humming the tune of: 'Three German officers crossed the Rhine, parley-vous?'. I couldn't remember all the words from those far-off days when we adolescent boys sang such songs for their naughtiness value on the top deck of the school bus, hoping to shock the girls who sat down below. It was a long time before I realised that the girls were way ahead of us boys in every respect, and all our singing did was prove what a bunch of dorks we really were.

I returned from my reverie to realise we had been winging along smoothly and effortlessly at 100mph on the autobahn for quite some time and without any kind of problem. We both kept our customary vigilance in the rear-view mirrors and had no trouble spotting overtaking cars in plenty of time. Yes, all the traffic moved fast, but provided you maintained good lane discipline and kept a regular mirror check, there was never going to be a problem with fast-approaching vehicles catching you unawares.

For Viv it was a revelation and all her fears were unfounded. When we stopped for lunch and fuel at the autobahn services, we both agreed that the UK motorways would be a lot better if we adopted the Germans' disciplined driving habits. On suitable roads it's not speed that's the problem. It's dopey and selfish drivers behaving in unpredictable ways that cause accidents.

The autobahns were a delight to ride, the miles clicked by and by 4pm we were approaching Munich in picture-postcard southern Bavaria. This was far enough for day three, so we took an *'ausfahrt'* (what a delightfully expressive word for a turn-off!) to Fürstenfeldbruck, mainly because I liked the name.

The town was as pretty as it sounded, but the receptionist at its central hotel said they had no vacancies and advised us to head off into the countryside to find accommodation. This sounded unlikely. Surely hotels would be in the towns, wouldn't they? I couldn't quite shake the idea that this might be a polite *'motorcyclists not welcome here'* message, but the girl appeared genuinely helpful, so we rode out of town, past butter-advert brown cows in picturesque meadows, with no real idea of where we were going or what we might find.

In the tiny hamlet of Hattenhofen I spotted the Gasthof Eberl-Fremdenzimmer, which I hoped meant a place to stay. My German is worse than my French, so as we pulled up I was less than confident. I searched my addled brain cells for a few words of German, not helped by my misspent youth reading war comics. All I could think of was *"Achtung, Spitfeuer!"* and *"Mein Gott! Der Tommis haf outvitted us again!"* None of which was likely to endear me to the locals.

Eventually I plucked up the courage to go inside and ask, *"Haben-sie ein doppelzimmer, bitte?"*

To which the very pretty young woman replied, *"Oh, would you like a room for the night?"* And I was both delighted and deflated in the same moment. How could she tell I was English? Then she offered to take me upstairs and show me the room and I decided I was much more delighted than deflated after all. Especially when she said the double room, together with breakfast, was only £25 for the pair of us. There's nothing quite like a bargain to get an old fella excited! I was so chuffed I booked us in for two nights.

As we struggled into the homely reception area with our bags, the young lady introduced herself as Victoria Eberl, the gasthof owner's daughter, and invited us to take a seat and rest for a while.

"I'm sure you would like a nice cool beer after all that riding!" she smiled, plonking a stein of foaming Bavarian brew in front of me, and treating Viv to her requested apple juice.

"I know how it feels," she said, *"I recently toured England and*

Ireland on the back of my boyfriend's motorbike. You need a beer at the end of the ride."

Ah, so that explained why she was so welcoming to two grubby bikers. But why was her English so excellent, while my German so bad?

"Maybe I paid attention at school?" she said with a knowing smile.

Beautiful, intelligent and with a great sense of humour – I was well impressed with our first fraulein of the trip. But Viv sensibly brought me back to earth with a nudge in the ribs.

"No, you can't take her home on the back of your motorbike," she said.

If we were pleased with the hotel and Victoria's warm welcome, we were knocked out by the sumptuous food in the restaurant that evening. We were served delicious meals, delightfully presented and again, very reasonably priced. We'd imagined that a choice little hotel in southern Bavaria would be mega-expensive, and couldn't believe our luck. Two nights here would be perfect, giving us a break from riding and a chance to visit Munich the next day.

With our washing line strung up at our bedroom window (can't take us anywhere) we settled down to sleep. The nearby church chimed every quarter hour through the night. After a fabulous meal and two large German beers, I slept like a log. Serenaded by my lusty snoring and the church bell's regular dongs, Viv dozed a little less soundly.

3

An Ugly Great Beast

Day 4, Sunday June 26th, Hattenhofen

Next morning I was up bright and early and washing bugs off the bikes before breakfast when a chap on an identical candy-orange Honda Varadero rode past, did a double-take, then came back for a natter. Well, as much of a natter as you can have between two bike enthusiasts who speak hardly a word of each other's language.

With lots of pointing, nods, smiles and *"sehr guts"*, we established that we both believed we owned the best bike in the universe. After giving me a hearty shoulder slap and handshake, he roared off down the road with a wave. It has to be said that his six foot two inches (I'm guessing here, height was way beyond my vocabulary) was more suited to this bike than my puny five foot six. How I came to buy one still seems improbable, all these years later.

It was spring 1999 and Viv and I had recently got back into biking. On our first holiday without our children in 25 years we'd gone a bit mad and hired a little motorbike to explore the hidden delights of Turkey. We had so much fun we decided to get a bike back home so we could grow old disgracefully. A few weeks later an old Honda 600 Revere put a smile on our faces and a crease in our backsides.

If we were going to do much more motorcycling, we needed something much more comfortable. We had test rides on lots of nice bikes but nothing really seemed to suit us. And then at a Honda roadshow in Norwich I spotted the newly-launched Varadero up on the stage and said to Viv:

"Cor, look at that ugly great beast! Let's go and take a closer look."

The 1000cc V-twin Varadero, named after a Cuban seaside resort and almost as big, had caused the media to coin a new phrase – 'monster trail bike' – and it was generally regarded as something of a joke by the UK motorcycling press. Impossibly tall, bulky and ungainly, they couldn't see anyone going for this new machine from Honda. But the bike press also seemed obsessed with race-replica sportsbikes, which had such extreme and excruciating riding positions, they would be a shortcut to the chiropractor for a middle-aged couple like us. What did they know?

So it was purely out of curiosity that we went up on stage to inspect this hulking great brute of a bike. A local dealer saw us approaching and pounced...

"Like the look of the new Varadero, Sir?" he asked. *"Jump on board and try it for size."*

"You must be joking," I replied. *"I'd need a step ladder to get up there!"*

"Try sitting in the saddle, Sir. You'll be surprised at what happens."

So I slung a leg up and over the broad seat, slithered my bum on to its soft padding and to my amazement the bike sank down on its suspension so that I could just get the tips of my toes to the ground.

"Now, Madam," the dealer turned to Viv, *"if you would like to hop on the pillion you can get an idea of how luxurious it feels on the road."*

Oh, he was good, this chap. With Viv on the back, the bike sank down even further and I could get the balls of both feet on the ground to hold us upright. Just. It felt great, in an intimidating sort of way.

"There. You won't find a more comfortable motorcycle for two-up touring," he said. *"Why not pop over to our showroom tomorrow and take our demonstrator out for a spin?"*

Quite why we turned up at the dealers the next day to ride a bike that was clearly too big for me and way out of our price range, I still don't know. But something drew us there and within minutes we were sitting astride a massive, throbbing machine at the kerbside, me wondering if I ever dare set off down the road on it. After I'd asked Viv for the third time if she was ready, and for the third time she'd answered *"Yes!"*, I couldn't put it off any longer. I let out the clutch and launched us on a magic carpet ride.

The second we pulled away, the huge and cumbersome bike lost all its bulk, became perfectly balanced and light as a feather to steer. The big V-twin engine woofled quietly as the scenery slipped by ever faster, and instantly I felt like I'd been riding this bike all my life. As Viv's arms wrapped around my waist, the Honda surged forward in a smooth rush of liquid power and the bike glided over the road's undulations as if they were made of treacle, not tarmac.

With knees nestled in large recesses in the tank, bums sunk deep in the sumptuous seat and the fairing deflecting the slipstream around us, I felt we were sitting *in* the bike as much as on it. A touch of the throttle and we were swept forward instantly. A touch of the brakes and the bike slowed rapidly without drama. The Varadero loved leaning through bends and the handling was perfect. It felt safe, effortless and supremely comfortable.

There was only one problem… I had to give it back!

The same smiling chap who had enticed us into the saddle the day before had sent us off on our morning test ride with a pat on my shoulder and these words: *"Go as far as you want. Just try to bring it back before we close at six o'clock tonight."*

He knew what he was doing. As the miles slid by and our grins spread ever further across our faces, the big Honda charmed its way into our affections. By the time we eventually returned to the shop and reluctantly prised ourselves out of its armchair comfort, I was in love. I couldn't stop stroking the tank and gazing at its voluptuous bodywork. Viv was equally smitten with the pillion ride. We were sold. We even signed up for colour-matched, Honda original equipment topbox and panniers and I barely seemed to notice as the bill soared to double our original bike budget.

This was most unlike me. I don't mind admitting to being careful with money. I simply don't enjoy spending it unnecessarily. I happily drive a tired old banger of a car, I'm comfortable in clothes from a charity shop and I can see no sense in buying something new when a perfectly good second-hand version is available at half the price.

But the Varadero wasn't available second-hand. It had just been launched and the first few had arrived in the country only weeks before. I had to have one. Now. Caution, reason and money flew out of the window hand in hand. And to this day I don't regret a single penny I spent on my lovely,

lovely Varadero. As far as I could tell, my new German biking buddy, fast disappearing from Hattenhofen on his identical Honda, felt exactly the same way.

Sunday 26th June had been designated a rest day, so we enjoyed a leisurely breakfast of home-made cheese, ham and other succulent cold meats. The Eberls also run a top-notch dairy and butcher's shop next door to the gasthof, with a farm out the back, so you couldn't get fresher or tastier food if you tried. Served with a variety of breads, jam, tea and coffee, we were set up for the day.

As we munched our way through this delightful feast, we were amused to see the cream of Hattenhofen's young men strutting around outside the restaurant across the street, fully kitted up in their lederhosen, braces and hats with feathers in, each downing a couple of litres of beer for breakfast before setting off for a bit of traditional Bavarian leg-slapping. And they didn't seem the least bit embarrassed at looking like a right bunch of twonks. Lest this sound like a racist slur, let me add that, in my opinion, English Morris Dancers look every bit as dopey, with an additional effeminate twist, but I'm very pleased both these yodelling and dwyle-flonking traditions are maintained as a poke in the eye for Euro conformity.

We asked Victoria if it would be possible to leave the bikes at the hotel and visit Munich by bus. No bus, she said, but she would take us in her car to the next village, Nannhofen, where we could catch the train. We protested unconvincingly for a few seconds, as we Brits are supposed to do, before accepting her generous offer graciously. She even helped us buy the right tickets from a machine at the unmanned station, and showed us the phone box where we could call for a taxi on our way back. What a sweetheart! Even Viv was beginning to see the attraction of taking her home with us.

The train was punctual, clean and efficient and delivered us to Munich city centre in time to see the 'glockenspiel' display of life-sized moving characters performing their animated routine on the hour in the clock tower of the gothically magnificent Ratthaus (town hall). Then Munich centre was taken over by a running marathon and we beat a hasty retreat to the botanical gardens where we could cool our feet in the fountain and write postcards home.

Ornate architecture delights the senses in Munich

After our impressive hotel breakfast, and anticipating another sumptuous banquet in the Eberl's restaurant that evening, we made do with an ice-cream for lunch. The afternoon was spent aimlessly wandering around the beautiful city, sight-seeing and people-watching, until our legs grew tired and we hopped back on the train which delivered us effortlessly to Nannhofen. By this stage we were feeling rather smug at our handling of the German transport system, and I fairly swaggered into the phone box to call a taxi. Two minutes later I slunk out of the phone box feeling feeble and foolish.

The Ratthaus features animated manikins on the hour

Lulled by Victoria's impeccable English, it hadn't occurred to me that I might not know how to call a taxi from a German phone box. I'd assumed there'd be dozens of cards for taxi companies, plus various other dubious services, stuck up all over the inside of the phone box in the kind of sleazy, commercial graffiti we find in the UK. But this was Germany. Clean. Efficient. No nonsense. No cards. No phone book.

There was, I'm sure, some simple means of finding a taxi if you knew how to navigate the phone's automated information system. But after several bewildering conversations with a syrupy-voiced fraulein, who turned out to be a series of recorded messages in undecipherable German, I finally gave up and admitted to Viv that we were stuck in a deserted railway station, miles from anywhere, without the first idea how to get back to our hotel.

Fortunately, we did have the number for our gasthof, where thankfully Victoria picked up the phone (her Dad doesn't speak a word of English). I asked if she could call a taxi for us, as we were stymied by lack of phone numbers and language. She said to wait there and she would get someone to us within a few minutes. So we read the timetable from top to bottom, raced each other up and down the three steps to the platform a few times and Viv slapped down my outstretched arm as I was preparing to launch into my best goose-stepping Hitler routine.

"Don't be so stupid!" she hissed. *"You don't know who could be watching us. You'll get us arrested and taken away in a blue van instead of a taxi."*

"Jahwohl, herr Commandant!" I replied, with a crisp nod and a click of my heels, then: *"Arrggh!"* as I discovered that flip flops were not the ideal footwear for this sort of tomfoolery. I was still rubbing my bruised ankles when a small car pulled up. It was Victoria.

"The taxis I called were all too expensive for you (she seemed to have an uncanny grasp of our low-budget lifestyle) *and too slow. They would take 30 minutes to get here, so I came myself,"* she said with a smile.

We felt very guilty for using her as an unpaid taxi service – she flatly refused all offers of petrol money – especially when she told us she was on her way out for the night, as the hotel was officially closed. We would have to go in through the back door to get to our room, and eat in the restaurant across the road that evening.

This last bit of news came as a bit of a blow, as we'd spent most of the day salivating at the thought of another gastronomic delight at the Gasthof Eberl. But we need not have worried, as the restaurant opposite did us proud and had two outstanding points in its favour. These were evident as we were welcomed by another attractive young lady, who seemed in a constant state of excitement while dashing to and fro with foaming steins of lager for the lederhosen lads, who were back from their leg-slapping duties and had obviously worked up a thirst.

After an equally knock-out nosh up of roast pork and chicken schnitzel, very tasty Sauerkraut and amazing potato creations, we were once again 'totally stonkered' and well impressed with Bavarian cuisine. We even got the restaurant owner and his mates to show us on our map the best route for our next day's ride over the Alps. All very friendly and helpful.

Then, on the way out, I took a closer look at the photo-portraits which covered the restaurant walls and discovered they were all the town's young men who had fought and died in their U-boats and Panzers in the last war. Just as well I didn't get too silly on the Bavarian brew and try out my Basil Fawlty 'greet the Germans' routine here, eh?

Day 5, Monday June 27th, Hattenhofen

In an effort to beat the heat, we fired up the bikes early and got rolling at 7am next day, taking the autobahn north around Munich, then east towards Salzburg, and finally south for the Alps. We soon crossed the border into Austria and had to buy 'vignettes', motorway toll stickers, in the service station. These gave us 10 days unfettered use of the Austrian autobahns for just £3 each, which would have been a bargain, but since we would be turning off the motorway in 6 miles, and were leaving Austria that afternoon, it all seemed a bit unnecessary.

I had a plan to cross the Alps via the Grossglockner Pass, which sounded good and looked suitably impressive on my little map, skirting a peak of 3797 metres. But first we had to find the turn for Kitzbühel, the internationally-famous ski-resort, where televised winter sports are broadcast to the world. You would suppose that the region's major tourist resort would justify some sort of signage from the nearby motorway, but no. We were halfway to Innsbruck before we realised we'd gone way too far, turned around at Schwaz and headed back north. Maybe we would get our money's worth out of our vignettes after all?

Still no signs. Still no Kitzbühel turning. After an hour and countless miles wasted trailing up and down the motorway, we finally decided to turn off into the little hamlet of Wordl and ask for directions, a man's least favoured option when he's lost. My anger and frustration soon evaporated as we followed the pointed finger and shortly after rode into the picture-postcard prettiness of Kitzbühel and found ourselves surrounded by gingerbread houses. Pottering about as if in a film set were old chaps in lederhosen, knitted socks and waistcoats, most accompanied by Heidi's grandma with plaits wrapped around her head.

The route from Kitzbühel up into the mountains was equally jaw-dropping, its steep green hillsides tinkling with the sound of cowbells. I half expected to see Julie Andrews leaping about to the sound of music and serenading the big, butch bikers coming the other way. This is a popular route with motorcyclists, we discovered, thanks to its sweeping bends and delightful views, and we met lots of leather-clad Harley riders bringing big grins down from the mountains.

It's easy to wave to riders on the continent, because there's no throttle on the passing side, so most bikers indulge in a friendly acknowledgment of their fellows with a left-handed flourish. All except the French riders, who have developed a national habit of waving their foot instead.

It's official: Viv's Honda Transalp goes over the Austrian Alps

Catching our breath after the
Felbertauern Tunnel on the Grossglockner Pass

As we neared the peaks of the snow-capped mountains, the pressure-cooker temperatures of the lowlands slipped away and it was deliciously cool when we stopped at the entrance to the Felbertauern Tunnel to snap a photo to validate Viv's bike's trans-Alpine credentials. After five days of unbearable heat, it was great to soak up the craggy, snow-covered scenery with waterfalls cascading down vertical cliffs, and inhale the cool, fresh, pine-scented air.

In the tunnel the atmosphere was instantly transformed into a thick, hazy fug, blue with exhaust fumes from the endless stream of cars and lorries passing through. We tried to breathe as little of it as possible on the one mile passage through to the southern side, where we stopped again to clear our lungs, check the map and update our route notes.

A curious elderly Austrian chap saw me working on the Varadero with a marker pen and came over to investigate. On the top of my bike's broad petrol tank I had taped a laminated A4 sheet of white paper – a home-made, flexible dry-wipe board – on which I jotted the road names and towns along our route for easy reference while on the move. On a bike, it's much too tedious to keep stopping to consult the road atlas, and far too dangerous to be riding along while trying to read a map through the clear map pocket of some tank-top bags. Take your eye off the road for many seconds and you're a goner!

But a quick glance at a boldly-written road number and the name of the next town keeps you on the right track. It seemed an obvious solution to me, but was clearly a new one on this bloke...

"Englisher?" he asked, as he watched me wipe away the morning's route and jot down the afternoon's directions. *"Ferry kleffer!"* he said, tapping the tank with a bony finger. It was not so kleffer when I accidentally brushed the board with my gloved hand as we set off and promptly erased half the route. Doh!

A few miles further down the mountain and we stopped again among the flower-sprinkled high meadows near Matrei in Osttirol for a picnic lunch of the rolls, ham and cheese liberated from Pa Eberl's breakfast that morning. We'd justified this dastardly theft on the basis that there's not much food you can force down at 6.30am, and his grub was far too tasty to leave behind.

The sun was bright, but the air still cool at 2000 metres before we descended to Lienz, heading east down the Drau Valley into the heat once more. This is prime country for spotting amusing place names, our childish way of raising a smile on long journeys. We passed Moos, a tiny village appropriately surrounded by dun cows munching grass, then Going, an ideal place, perhaps, for those who've not quite settled down, and finally my favourite, Giggleweg.

Then it was time to pay full attention to traffic on a last stretch of autobahn for the hot dash south to the Slovenian border, crossed via another smoky tunnel, this one 2.85 miles long. By the time we emerged, coughing and spluttering, into the fierce afternoon heat of northern Slovenia we were totally knackered and grabbed the chance to stop at the first service area for fuel, water and currency exchange.

So far we'd been in the Euro zone, but now we needed to change some Sterling for Slovenian Tolars, which Viv promptly renamed 'Toenails'. This was her own type of currency conversion, designed to help us remember the name of the local lucre. Otherwise there was a real risk we'd call everything spondulicks.

It was baking hot as we slumped next to our bikes and slurped a couple of litres of bottled water in an attempt to cool down, the chill of the mountains long forgotten. Slovenian families were splashing themselves with water from the service station's outdoor tap, in between filling up any containers they could find to sustain them on their journeys. It looked like their Ladas didn't have air conditioning either.

While we tried to cool down, we referred to our pre-trip notes for clues to the protocol for this former Yugoslavian country. It seemed we could expect heavy, on-the-spot fines for any traffic offences or jaywalking, and there was a zero tolerance policy on drink driving. This suited us, as we were never tempted to mix alcohol and motorcycling, and if all the other drivers were sober there was a greater chance of us getting through the country in one piece.

However, we took this information with a pinch of salt. In our experience, zero tolerance is often code for zero enforcement. Countries with ineffectual policing usually try to make up for a lack of coppers on the beat by imposing outrageous sentences on the one per cent of offenders who do get caught.

What else did we know about Slovenia? The forest areas were allegedly riddled with tick-borne encephalitis, which would discourage any Ray Mears-type impromptu wild camping. And the word for thank you was *"Hvala"*.

This was all the information our tired and overheated brains could cope with. Which was just as well. It was all we had. So we dragged ourselves upright again, shrugged on our sweaty jackets and helmets and pointed our Hondas towards Bled. This town with the unfortunate name was chosen because it was the nearest and we were too exhausted to ride any further, having covered 350 hot and sticky miles since Hattenhofen.

It was a happy choice, as Bled turned out to be a charming lake-side resort and within minutes we'd found a room for the night in a lovely three-storey wooden chalet. Svigelj Sobe (rooms) had its first floor ringed with one long geranium-bedecked balcony, and Pa Svigelj directed us to lock our bikes up in his ornate wooden garage, all natural timbers and cute little peek-a-boo windows.

Once again we were exhausted after 13 hours on the road – the last few in unbearable heat – and after a shower we barely had the strength to stagger down the steep hill leading to beautiful Lake Bled. We agreed we would appreciate the view better after a night's rest, so trudged back up the hill, pausing only for a snack pizza in the crazy golf café, before falling into our welcoming beds.

Fairytale castles overlook beautiful Lake Bled in Slovenia

4

Bitten and Bled

Day 6, Tuesday June 28th, Bled

We awoke refreshed after a good night's sleep, but badly bitten after sleeping naked and uncovered next to the open window. Fortunately it was mosquitoes, not vampires to blame (we were still a couple of days away from Transylvania), a hazard of hot summer nights beside the lake.

The cockerels were still crowing as we went through our usual morning routine: we'd both shower, have a hot drink and whatever food we'd saved for breakfast in our room. Then I would take a bottle of water down to wash the bugs off our bikes' screens and lights and return with the bike locks. These were two chunky disc-locks that stopped the front wheels from turning, plus a hefty safety chain which looped through the rear wheels. None of these would stop a professional thief, but we hoped they would deter the casual joy rider. If nothing else, they provided us with peace of mind.

By the time I got back to the room Viv would have finished the packing and we'd struggle down the stairs with the cases and bags, jackets and helmets. With the luggage installed on the bikes and the route updated on my *"ferry kleffer"* tank-top dry-wipe board, we'd be ready to rock.

As Viv paid our landlord for our night's excellent lodgings, he said, *"Go carefully, young lady,"* which put a smile on her face for the start of the day.

After a photo-stop by the lake – tranquil and beautiful, surrounded by steep wooded hills and fairy-tale castles on high peaks – we pressed on following the minor route

41

across Slovenia that Pa Svigelj had recommended. From Bled we passed through Kranj (pronounced Kran), then to Kamnik and Melnik along a lovely twisty road through gorgeous countryside. We rode through densely wooded hills with farms perched prettily on top, picturesque wooden farm houses flanked by elaborate timber sheds and wood stores, all constructed with artistic flair and enhancing the landscape.

There were other amazing structures on every farm: tall wooden frames festooned with hay. Again, these all seemed to conform to a national blueprint, with 12-15 foot high uprights supporting two, three or four horizontal crossbars over which the grasses were hung to dry in the sun.

Every farmstead was spick and span, with not a single abandoned tractor or rusting farm implement to be seen anywhere. It was as if the picture-postcard landscape had inspired the population to aesthetic excellence. We decided we must revisit this tiny but delightful country, when we had the time to appreciate it more fully.

With two more countries to discover before the day was out, we pressed on and as we neared the eastern end of Slovenia found we couldn't avoid a short stretch of motorway. This extracted two tolls from us before the turn off for Ptuj (pronounced Tui) and the border with Croatia.

The landscape was flatter here, with no pretty farmsteads to brighten up the scenery, as we passed Ormosz on our way out of the country. There was one last fuel station, conveniently situated just before the border, allowing us to fill the bikes' tanks and grab a bite of lunch using up the last of our Toenails.

Worryingly, Viv had developed a serious backache which had spread to her arms making them quite numb. This was far from ideal when riding a heavy and powerful motorcycle. I gave her a stand-up massage which rubbed enough feeling back into her upper limbs for us to carry on into Croatia, but she was clearly very uncomfortable.

As soon as we crossed the border into the next country, every house looked scruffy and unkempt and the people impoverished. But it was a brief glimpse as we crossed the northern tip of Croatia and within 30 miles were in Hungary, where they were still driving Wartburgs, which was a trip down memory lane.

Twenty five years earlier, while living in Dorset, we had owned and loved a shiny blue Wartburg estate car. After a succession of tired old bangers, the reliability and practicality of this East German car, with its distinctive three-cylinder, two-stroke engine, suited our young family and my limited budget.

We had soon got used to the 'ring-a-ding, ding, ding' of the exhaust whenever we took a foot off the throttle, and the clouds of blue smoke when accelerating, especially up hills. I dare say if we drove one today its idiosyncrasies would horrify us, but seeing these bumbling cars again, ring-a-ding-dinging along in a haze of blue smoke, filled us with nostalgia as well as exhaust fumes. They didn't look out of place wobbling along between bulbous old trucks that were coughing out obliterating smokescreens of black diesel smoke. It was immediately obvious that Hungary was some way behind environmentally-conscious Western Europe on green issues.

It was now mid-afternoon and the heat, humidity and choking exhaust fumes forced us to pull in to a fuel station in Nagykanizsa for a break. Which was just as well, as Viv was really suffering now and slumped to the ground in the shade of the shop front and burst into tears. The pain in her back, numbness in her arms and the heat and exhaustion were just too much and she was about done in, poor girl.

I left her in the shade sipping a bottle of water while I blatted into town looking for an ATM in order to extract some local currency – 20,000 Hungarian Fiorints costing around £80. Back at the garage, after a cereal bar and another back massage, Viv said she would be able to do a few more slow and cautious miles in order to reach Lake Balaton, where, we figured, we should be able to find a bed for the night.

It was only 25 miles to Balatonkeresztúr, but this was plenty far enough on badly deformed roads, deeply furrowed by the endless thunder of heavy trucks, especially when the heavens opened with a shower of fat raindrops. Turning off the main highway we spotted a hotel and pulled on to its forecourt with a sigh of relief.

This was speedily followed by a sigh of frustration, as the hotel was full. The news made Viv slump over her handlebars in pain and tears, her hands too numb to grip any more. She was at the end of her tether and riding around town looking for another place to stay was out of the question. Standing beside her wondering what to do, the rain rattling on my helmet, I spotted a house over the road with a sign outside saying: 'sobe/zimmer/apt' which sounded promising, so I set off to investigate.

My knock was answered by a pleasant German lady, which was handy, because if my German is poor, my Hungarian is non-existent. She led me down the garden path – literally – to the bottom of her delightfully green and pleasant property. There, across neat lawns and beneath dripping fruit trees, was an immaculate new semi-detached bungalow – ours for just £20 a night! Inside was a huge lounge with satellite TV, fully-equipped kitchen and dining area, two bedrooms, a bathroom and an additional loo. I immediately booked us in for two nights, hoping a rest day in this peaceful and luxurious retreat would help Viv's back recover.

While Viv attempted to soak her aches away in the tub, I walked to the nearby co-operative shop to buy sausages, pasta, carrots and cabbage, figuring a good meal would help restore our flagging spirits. I cooked while Viv rested on the sumptuous bed, tried to return her spine and shoulders to some sort of normality and get the life back into her hands and arms.

As I stirred the steaming pots I ran through our options in my mind. If there wasn't a marked improvement in her condition we'd have to call off the trip. Riding home would be as impossible for her as continuing eastwards. I'd have to put Viv on a flight from Budapest and find a way to get her bike shipped home, before turning my Varadero around and riding back across Europe on my own. Not a happy prospect.

Luxury rest stop at Balatonkeresztúr in Hungary

Chapter 4

Day 7, Wednesday June 29th, Balatonkeresztúr

What a difference a good night's sleep makes. After a blissful 10 hours of comfort and silence we awoke to blue skies and bright sunshine. Viv's back and shoulders were still fairly stiff, but the numbness had gone from her arms and her hands were working again. She felt sure she'd be ready to ride again after another day and night of rest.

It looked like the trip was back on, so I grabbed the opportunity to give the bikes a thorough check over. Viv's Transalp was low on oil, which was unusual as it hardly drinks a drop normally, and the Varadero was low on coolant. This was more understandable after the fiercely hot weather of the past week and was easy to remedy with a quarter litre of tap water, but the Transalp needed half a litre of the best 15-40W oil a nearby garage could provide, in order to reach the top of its dipstick.

By now it was mid-morning and my head was burning under the scorching Hungarian sun. I needed some protection if I was going to finish my work on the bikes without getting sunstroke. Draping a bath towel over my head and shoulders did the trick and I thought I looked rather dashing, like Lawrence of Arabia. That bubble burst when Viv collapsed in fits of laughter at the sight of my headgear, which probably helped ease the tension between her shoulder blades as much as it protected me from sunstroke.

Attempting to keep the pristine white towel clean while I lubed the chains (no more tension worries here, thank goodness), I also checked the tyres, lights, brake fluids, controls and cables. All were okay. What was causing me concern was my Varadero's fairing. This had been cracked six years previously when I lost my footing at a standstill and couldn't hold the big brute up with all its luggage fitted. The result was a few annoying scratches and a crack that had never caused any trouble because other parts of the fairing held it all together.

All had been well until the fateful service just before this trip, when the retaining lugs holding together the side of the fairing and centre cowling had been broken off. I'd noticed this just before we set off, but with no time to get it fixed, I decided to ignore it and hope it wouldn't become a problem. Now, after 1500 miles on increasingly rough roads, my fairing was threatening to part company with the bike. Something had to be done.

Equipped with only the bike's toolkit, my trusty Leatherman multi-tool and a few bits of bent wire (which no adventure motorcyclist should ever leave home without), I spent the next hour and a half making holes, threading wires and twisting them together to effect a repair. It was not pretty, but it was very strong. I hoped it would last the journey.

Later we walked through the town with the intention of having a stroll along the shores of Lake Balaton, the largest in Central Europe and a top tourist destination. Due to Hungary being landlocked, this is affectionately called the 'Hungarian Sea' and it stretches for 48 miles alongside our road to Budapest. But we were thwarted as all the shore-side land is privately owned and fenced off. Unless you stay in one of the resort's lakeside hotels, all you get to see is a distant glimpse of water through the trees.

So we amused ourselves by buying postcards and provisions, plus vignettes – our toll tokens – for the Hungarian motorways that we would use while approaching and circumnavigating Budapest the following day, all being well. Viv's back and shoulders had improved steadily throughout the day and she was confident she would be good to go. We settled up with our landlady and got an early night with a view to hitting the road at 6am next day.

5

In The Groove

Day 8, Thursday June 30th, Balatonkeresztúr

It was cloudy and damp and pleasantly cool as we rattled through more villages alongside the seemingly endless Lake Balaton next morning. Many of these towns had modern tidy villas owned by Germans, if the car registrations were any guide, but other hamlets had a distinctly Hungarian feel, filled with plain houses, portly chaps and baggy women heading to work in the fields.

Several turns for the motorway were blanked off, which was frustrating, as we were keen to get off the worn out, slick and lumpy single carriageway and get some more comfortable miles under our wheels. But much of the motorway that was marked on our map had not yet been built. I was concerned that the extra effort needed to ride these rutted and undulating old tarmac roads was putting additional strain on Viv's back, so was relieved when we finally gained access to the dual carriageway that we had bought vignettes for and were able to increase our pace.

By 7.30am we were on the outskirts of Budapest, the Hungarian capital, dicing with rush-hour traffic on the M0, the southern ring road, a two-lane version of London's M25. It came with a similarly scaled down service area where we were able to refuel the bikes and breakfast on coffee and cakes.

Suitably fortified, we set off again following the garage man's helpful instructions (thank goodness so many people speak a little English!) and were soon clear of the city traffic, heading east across fertile flatlands towards Romania.

Our delight at being out in the country was tempered by the woeful state of the tarmac.

Once the motorway ended, the road deteriorated rapidly, with appallingly rutted and bumpy surfaces, beaten to a pulp by a thousand lorries each day. The grooves worn by their wheels were so deep that you took your life in your hands when trying to cross the furrows to overtake the smoke-belching trucks. But staying behind these overladen juggernauts that were bumping and grinding along at 40mph was not an option if we were going to reach our destination in reasonable time that day.

Climbing over the ridge in the centre of the road and dropping into the offside furrow in order to overtake, made my bike sway and wobble. Re-crossing the ridges after passing the truck was even worse, as increased speed turned a wobble into a weave. Unbeknown to me, Viv was having an even worse experience, with her bike's high and heavy topbox acting like a pendulum causing her Transalp to weave horribly over the road grooves. She was reluctant to follow me for fear of losing control completely, but even more fearful of being left behind and lost in a foreign country.

Viv's no slouch when it comes to overtaking. Thanks to some excellent training with Norfolk's motorcycle cops shortly after getting her Honda, she took to heart their principles of *'forward planning and observation'* and is good at *'making progress'* as the police bikers describe carving through the traffic. Consequently, Viv has no problem judging speed, distance and opportunity and makes confident, safe overtakes – usually singing Steve Winwood's *"While you see a chance, take it"* as she goes.

So it was especially frustrating to see me disappearing while she was unable to follow due to the awful road destabilising her bike. Eventually she realised that if she hung back I would get the message that something was wrong. When she vanished from my rear view mirrors I pulled over until she caught up and was able to explain her dilemma. The tension was beginning to lock up her shoulders again.

We agreed to slow down until we came to better road surfaces where overtaking would be less of a heart-stopping manoeuvre, but it seemed that wouldn't be anytime soon. As we headed further east, the look and feel of the towns we passed through slid progressively down the affluence scale.

Wartburgs and Trabants made more regular appearances, bumping, weaving and spluttering along, coughing blue smoke into the atmosphere.

What the towns and villages lacked in grandeur they more than made up for in unpronounceability. After Törökszentmiklós, we slipped past Kisújszállás and Püspökladány before pulling in to a fuel station in Berettyóújfalu for petrol, to stretch our legs and shoulders and grab a late lunch. Viv's shoulders were sore, but no arm numbness so far, thank goodness.

Despite my concerns about slow progress, we were only about half an hour from the Romanian border, which was a relief, as our destination was Oradea, a similar distance the other side. Local motorists, noticing our GB stickers and unusual registration plates, quizzed us in several languages before they twigged we were English, and then their curiosity turned to amazement at our riding bikes such a distance.

"England – you?" asked one chap in a shell suit who sported equal length stubble on chin and scalp. Then, nodding at Viv in disbelief, *"Womans driving mottorad all from England?! Wah!"*

The garage proprietor was less astounded, as he owned a V-Strom, Suzuki's version of my Varadero, and he knew what these machines could do. We'd seen a lot of these big V-twins in Slovenia and Hungary, a tribute to Suzuki's marketing and their machines' suitability for these challenging continental roads. Sportsbikes, so popular in the UK for the past few years, would be virtually unrideable on these corrugated surfaces, we reckoned.

By mid-afternoon we were being waved through Hungarian customs, but there was a long queue on the Romanian side as the officials scrutinised the documents of everyone entering from the decadent west. Finally our passports were stamped, our sheaves of bike papers returned and we rode into Romania.

Immediately the country looked – and smelled – different. Odd chemicals, burning plastics and rubber plus untreated sewage assaulted our senses in the scruffy border hamlets and we felt we'd entered the Third World. We had hardly taken in our new surroundings before we were entering Oradea, a sizeable city, and were instantly overwhelmed by four lane, nose-to-tail traffic, tramlines criss-crossing the road and a welter of bewildering signs. Help! What do we do now?

Again fat warm raindrops began to fall so we opted out of the chaos and confusion of Oradea's main drag, and pulled into the forecourt of a posh hotel. We were due to meet up with EveryChild's staff in this city and there had been a suggestion that we may be offered accommodation too, so we needed to make contact before we got swallowed up by the swirling traffic and lost. Maybe this swanky hotel could help?

I felt distinctly out of place, shuffling into the plush, red-carpeted foyer in my riding gear. After more than a week on the road I was dirty and dishevelled and the last minute rain had not improved my appearance, as rivulets of water streaked my dusty jacket.

Fortunately, Anca the receptionist at Hotel Scorilo – tall, blonde and looking like a fashion model – didn't bat an eyelid and gave us a warm welcome when I explained our predicament.

In perfect English she said, *"No problem. Perhaps you would like me to call your friends for you? Then you can arrange to meet up."* She finished with a film-star smile. Mmm, if all the women in Romania were as pretty and helpful as Anca, maybe the country had more going for it than I'd thought...

We called the charity's local office and spoke to our contact Ady, who said she would drive over to meet us and guide us to our accommodation in half an hour or so. Cushty. Then our dishy receptionist suggested we parked our bikes in the hotel's inner courtyard, where they'd be away from jealous eyes, and treated ourselves to a coffee in the 'garden terrace' restaurant, while she looked after our helmets and jackets for us. What a sweetheart!

Anca surprised us both by enthusing about our bikes and said she hoped to get a scooter one day. Although her looks suggested a Ferrari might be more appropriate, in Romania, it seemed, one's ambitions needed to be tempered by the financial reality of the country. No wonder so many Romanian women leave to seek their fortunes elsewhere.

I was just considering whether we needed a receptionist back home and how much a scooter might cost, when Viv nudged me in the ribs and said: *"If you can drag yourself away, I'm ready for that coffee now."* Could she read my mind?

Compared to the houses nearby, Hotel Scorilo was a haven of opulence and an island of comfort and peace in a sea of turbulent traffic. The garden restaurant featured smart, uniformed waiters and an extensive menu in English, which started with *'Welcome your Excellency...'*. If they thought our appearance fell a little short of their desired standard, they didn't show it, and brought us two delicious coffees and two bottles of water to help us unwind, rehydrate and recaffeinate after our long and trying day on the road. We'd been riding for 10 hours, but due to the road conditions and traffic hazards it felt more like 20 and we were cream-crackered.

While we soaked up our liquids, we learned a little more about this small but high-class establishment. Built in 1703, originally as a bishop's residence, Hotel Scorilo claimed to interlace tradition with innovation: *'guest rooms have last minute endowment... exactly to satisfy the taste of the most exigent customers'*. Meanwhile the restaurant offered *'The most divers menus, the most rafinated cocktails,'* and *'an informatised system of taking the orders from the moment they are requested'*.

We suppressed a smile with the thought that if we had to write a hotel's blurb in Romanian, it would not be rafinated at all. In fact the sum total of our grasp of the language was *'multi mesc'* (thank you), which might prove insufficient. A quick check of our pre-trip notes warned us to beware of bogus policemen, illegal money changers on the streets, and stray dogs that carried rabies and African typhus. Gulp.

Before we could start to panic, Ady and her colleague Claudia, both young, slim brunettes, arrived in a battered old Dacia car with half-flat tyres. Claudia didn't speak English but she could drive their rusty old bus, while Ady spoke very good English but didn't drive. It would be handy having two in the car, I thought, for when they needed to push, which looked like it could be any minute. EveryChild obviously don't waste their donors' money on luxury limos for regional staff. As we'd seen in Malawi, and were soon to discover here in Eastern Europe, they channel every possible penny in to helping the people who need it. Which is excellent.

We followed the Dacia as it wobbled and weaved through the rush-hour traffic, right across town to a huge long residential block. On the seventh floor was an apartment we could use for a couple of nights while in town. Neat. But we couldn't leave the bikes here, said Ady.

"They will be stolen for sure. If you take your eyes off them for five minutes they will be gone, believe me," she said. And we did.

So after unloading all our gear and struggling up to the top floor in the ancient, groaning lift to deposit our luggage, we hopped back on the bikes to ride them to 44 Kogalniceanu Street, a secure parking lot consisting of a walled compound with 24-hour guards.

"If you have locks for your motorbikes, you should also fit them here," said Ady, as she noticed the couple of lads who were on guard duty were drooling at the sight of our shiny machines.

Only snag was, we'd left the locks in our panniers at the apartment. Doh! The girls were very patient, ferrying us to the monolithic apartment block to retrieve them, then returning me to the parking lot to fit them and pay the man 100,000 Romanian Lei – a little less than £2 Sterling!

We could afford to be a bit flash, as Viv and I were now millionaires, having exchanged €60 for 2,118,000 Lei on the way from our digs (and not at an illegal street money changer, honest officer… if you are an honest officer?). The exchange rate of 35,300 Romanian Lei to the Euro was only temporary, however. The next day the Lei was to devalue by four noughts, Ady told us, making €1 worth just 3.53 Lei. Unfortunately this didn't mean our newly-acquired spondulicks (Viv had yet to rename them) would be worth 10,000 times as much in the morning. It merely meant that every 10,000 Lei note would still be legal tender and worth exactly the same, but would now be <u>called</u> one Lei. Confused? We certainly were.

Eventually, after all the to-ing and fro-ing was over, our helpful and patient hosts left us to settle in to the EveryChild guest accommodation after arranging to pick us up in the morning for visits to the charity's projects nearby.

Time to catch our breath and look around our temporary home. The flat, as Ady called it, was spacious with kitchen, bathroom, lounge-diner and two bedrooms, all filled with an odd assortment of furniture still bearing numbered stickers from the auction where it had been purchased. It wasn't palatial, but we were very grateful for it.

The flat's seventh-floor position gave us excellent views over Oradea, with a busy four-lane road running alongside double tram tracks and a rattling textile mill to the front, and an electricity sub-station to the rear. Beyond to the north were the red tiled roofs and trees of a more affluent suburb leading to green hills, while to the south and west were many more apartment blocks, some of them ten storeys high.

*Four-lane highway and two-lane tramway
outside our Oradea apartment*

*Romanian skyline: textile factory (left) to the front
of our apartment…*

… and electricity sub-station to the rear, viewed from the 7th floor

We decided the kitchen was sufficiently well equipped for us to rustle up our own meal, so we set off on foot to find food. The earlier rain had cooled the temperature to a humid 27 degrees centigrade, a welcome relief from the recent 35 degrees, as we wandered around a nearby market.

Many of the Romany stall-holders were packing up (it was 6.30pm) and their language was incomprehensible – no English spoken here. Despite this we managed to buy fruit and veg, tinned tuna, cheese and an intriguing flat round bread, and still had 1.7 million Lei left. We quite liked being millionaires, if only for one brief evening.

Back at the flat we realised we didn't have any matches to light the gas cooker, so I rattled back down in the creaking, groaning lift and legged it to a nearby bar to buy a cigarette lighter. This proved surprisingly unsuitable for the job, burning our fingers while trying to light the rings, which were set low down in the hob and therefore required us to hold the lighter upside down – ouch!

We then went to plan B, lighting strips of twisted paper as tapers. After a few fumbled attempts which had me dancing the Pyromaniac Fling, these did the job but had the unwanted side effect of filling the kitchen with choking smoke. I had visions of approaching sirens, a ladder appearing outside our window and a jet of water dousing our supper, but a quick check of the apartment revealed no smoke alarms. Residents can set fire to themselves here without fear of being troubled by the Oradea fire brigade.

Having got the rings lit, Viv rummaged around in a drawer for cooking implements and immediately found a sparking gas ring lighter. What bright sparks we were!

Following a fine, if slightly unusual, meal helped down by half a bottle of Romanian Moscatel, we soon succumbed to the rigours of the day and slept soundly, despite the constant clatter of trams and textile bobbins outside the open window.

6

Cart Horses And Mafia

Day 9, Friday July 1st, Oradea

One advantage of hotels, we now realised, was they provide towels, something our borrowed apartment lacked. After her shower and a few minutes of frenzied activity, Viv appeared looking pink and pleased with herself. She announced that a flannel can work just as well as a towel, and all the rubbing and wringing provides early morning exercise too. What a resourceful girl I married!

We breakfasted on bread and apples before taking another stroll around the market to see how the stall-holders had coped with the overnight currency transition. They'd obviously been planning this for weeks – not one of the canny marketeers stumbled over their prices or change as we bought provisions for supper.

At 10.30am Ady and Claudia returned to take us on visits to various EveryChild projects. The journey was quite an experience, as the rear seats of the clapped-out Dacia 1310 (a Romanian-built copy of an ancient Renault) had no seat belts, the car's suspension pogoed like Zebedee at bedtime, and its tyres were still not inflated properly, despite my suggestion the day before that this might be advisable. With two extra passengers, the car now squirmed around like a jelly at a kids' party.

What with the badly surfaced roads, slippery tramlines and manic drivers around us we could only wonder, as we sat white-knuckled and gibbering in the back seat, how any vehicle made it to its destination in this country. Outside the city much of the local traffic was horse drawn, with lumbering great farm carts loaded with hay or manure pulled at walking pace by a single horse. These shared the narrow, beaten-up roads with smoke-belching trucks and new Mercedes cars with blacked-out windows driven by the region's Mafia. The latter were the real hazard, being driven at suicidal speeds and slowing down for nobody. It was like Mad Max meets Death Race 2000.

A few miles out of Oradea we came to the village of Tileagd where we visited an EveryChild 'Helping School' for children with learning disabilities. With old TV images in our minds of the desperate institutions which housed these kids in post-Ceaucescu Romania, we were pleasantly surprised by conditions here. Clean, bright dormitories housed these 7-16 year olds in smart bunk beds with fresh linen.

Attractive day rooms, with games and TV, would appeal to any western child. And in the crafts room were embroidered tablecloths, wall hangings and clothes, plus paintings and colourful decorated bowls, paperweights and other products of young hands and minds.

Crafts room in EveryChild's 'Helping School' in Tileagd, Romania

Besides teaching these arts and crafts, the school works hard to provide the children with life skills, such as cooking and sewing, and the kids also get pocket money so they learn financial skills and personal responsibility too. It's important, say EveryChild, to equip these young people for life in the real world.

The school is usually home to 120 boarding pupils, 77 of whom are orphaned or abandoned and have no families. The rest have families who can't afford to care for them at home. The school has 23 teaching staff plus 20 housekeeping staff, running the kitchens and laundry etc.

There used to be 240 kids here, but thanks to the hard work of EveryChild and other agencies, the Romanian government is now encouraging families to keep their disabled children at home and in local schools, where extra resources have provided for special-needs children. Wherever possible, the family is the best place for these children, say the charity. Institutions are not the answer, so they make every effort to support the families – often cash-strapped and poorly educated themselves – to care for their children at home. Some of this support is financial, much of it educational, but at every step the investment is in the child's future.

We left Tileagd for another wobbly ride back to Oradea, much encouraged by what we'd seen and eager to check out an EveryChild Community Centre in the city. But first we had an appointment with the press at the EveryChild office, organised by John, the charity's local manager.

Although we fell a long way short of the film-star status of Ewan and Charley, our arrival on motorcycles, all the way from Britain, was enough to summon up weekly and daily newspaper reporters, keen to find out what motivated us. They obviously don't get Hell's Grannies riding across the continent to support a charity in Romania every day.

Having been a newspaper reporter and magazine journalist in the past, I'd agreed to this press call without too much thought. But now the time had come, I was nervous. I suddenly remembered how intrusive and probing reporters can be, and how a misplaced word or phrase can quickly appear in headlines to haunt you for years to come.

As it turned out, the Romanian reporters were surprisingly courteous and considerate. Perhaps they realised they were dealing with a pair of dopey grandparents, not a couple of hardened bikers. After pumping us for our views of what we'd seen so far, and how we thought EveryChild were making a difference to the disadvantaged youngsters of their country, they closed their notebooks and left, no doubt to rush to their editors shouting, *"Hold the front page!"*. Or not.

Our arrival might have been less than earth-shattering news, but the charity was certain it would help to publicise their work and raise the profile of child care in Romania. Convincing the public as well as local and national government of the value of their children helped to change the country's old institutionalised thinking and bring about legislation reform, they said.

Next stop was a few miles across town to one of EveryChild's Community Centres, a top priority in the charity's campaign for supporting children and their families. Inside an unassuming building (no donors' cash wasted here either) we discovered a suite of rooms where an impressive array of services are provided – social workers, counsellors, psychologists, speech therapists, doctors, legal advisors – all aimed at helping families become better able to care for their children.

In some cases this might mean assisting with documentation for social help or fighting evictions. One common problem in post-communist Romania is former owners reclaiming the houses taken from them by the old communist regime. Which is all well and good, but the result is many poorer families face eviction, which invariably affects the welfare of children.

Teachers visit the centre regularly, providing extra lessons for up to 15 children, plus volunteers help with classes in English, French and computing, all helping to break the cycle of poverty, ignorance and poor education. Hard-up families can even bring their children into the centre for baths and to do their laundry, as many have only a hand pump in their gardens. One lady with seven children comes every Saturday to wash her kids and clothes, we were told.

By late afternoon our whirlwind tour of just a tiny part of EveryChild's Romanian activities was over and, suitably impressed, we were ferried back to our apartment by the ever-helpful Ady and Claudia. By now we were getting used to the hair raising ride in their battered old Dacia. It reminded us of our travels in Luxor, Egypt, with Alaa over a decade previously…

Our first trip to Africa in 1994 had been a real culture shock. We'd decided that a week's holiday to see the famous Egyptian temples and tombs at Luxor would be educational for us and our youngest son, Michael, then 11 years old. But we weren't really prepared for the frantic bustle of life beside the Nile.

Having rejected the tour company's many excursion offers at the first morning's 'welcome meeting' for being too organised, too boring and too expensive, we set out on foot from our hotel and were immediately mobbed by hundreds of excited Arabs wearing Wee Willie Winkie nightshirts, trying to sell us everything under the sun. Kaleshes (horse and cart rides), feluccas (sailboat trips) and dozens of ancient artefacts and modern commodities were thrust upon us by an endless throng of desperately earnest men who simply would not take 'no' for an answer.

We were overwhelmed by the insistent shouts and constant hassle of the crowd of hustlers who followed us along the pavement. We were about to turn and run back to the sanctuary of our hotel when a small plump man wearing thick glasses and western clothes stepped up to us and waved all the others away.

"Don't take any notice of them. My name is Alaa and I can help you to see everything you want by taking you in my car. Where would you like to go?" he asked.

We were so relieved to be rescued, we did a deal for the next three days, for Alaa to take us to see the sights. His car was on the other side of the Nile, so he would meet us at our hotel after breakfast and take us across the river in a motor launch and then drive us in his car to see the valleys of the Kings, Queens and Nobles, the tombs and the temples. We did the obligatory haggling, agreed a price and arranged to meet at 8am next day.

Alaa was waiting for us as we left the hotel's breakfast room, and escorted us to the river bank where a man with a boat was waiting. So far so good. After a ten-minute ride across the broad Nile, we scrambled up the far bank to find Alaa's car... and our jaws dropped.

Once upon a time this vehicle had been a white Peugeot, but that must have been back in the time of the Pharaohs. Now it was a dented, rusty, crumpled, decrepit scrap heap with rocks wedged in front and behind all four wheels.

We were aghast and stopped dead in our tracks.

"*Come, come,*" urged Alaa, waving us towards his old wreck. "*Please, sit inside and make yourselves comfortable.*" After a few hearty tugs he succeeded in wrenching open a rear door and ushered Viv and Michael on to the back seat. They both looked terrified as he slammed the door shut. He then attacked the front passenger door, which made an anguished screech of tortured metal as it opened, and with a flourish waved me towards a seat whose red plastic cover had been split and shredded by years of harsh sunlight.

As I sat down the wrecked seat shot backwards the full length of its rail and crashed into Mike's knees, unimpeded by the latch mechanism one normally associates with the front seats in cars. Alaa slammed the door shut and there seemed little prospect that we'd ever get out again, dead or alive.

He then went to the front of the car, propped the bonnet up on his shoulder and fiddled about for a minute, after which there were a couple of loud clunks as the engine was cranked over in protest. A few coughs and bangs and the motor rumbled into some semblance of life, while dense smoke arose around us from an exhaust system that was more holes than pipe.

Viv, who had been sitting in stunned and wide-eyed silence, found her voice: "*My God! Do you think this car is safe?*"

If God replied, he couldn't be heard over the clattering engine, so I offered her my best reassurance instead, "*I don't suppose there's any traffic here, and he's bound to drive slowly in this old bus. I'm sure we'll be okay.*" I didn't believe a word of it, but I couldn't think what else to do.

"*We'll have to open a window,*" said Viv, as she heaved on a seized-up window winder in vain, "*or we'll cook in here.*" Mike's side had no window handle at all, and my window was rusted shut, like Viv's.

Alaa had now lowered the bonnet and was twisting two bits of wire together to hold it down. He noticed our frenzied attempts to open a window and came to see what the problem was. I explained that we needed some air, but couldn't open the windows.

"*I will open the sun-roof,*" said Alaa, who proceeded to tug at the panel over our heads until it grudgingly moved a few inches, showering us with a blizzard of rust-flakes and dust and letting a strip of searing hot sunlight scorch my forehead.

Meanwhile, Mike had pushed my seat forward with his feet until my knees crashed into the remains of the dashboard, but when he relaxed, his legs folded and my seat shot back into the rear compartment again. With a sigh, Alaa climbed back out of the car, walked around to my side, picked up a large rock and snatched open my door.

I recoiled with a cowardly whimper, wondering if a beating with a rock was what befell all passengers who didn't sit still. But Alaa said, *"No, my friend. It is for the seat."* And proceeded to wedge the rock under my legs and the errant seat was fixed.

By now a crowd of small, dirty urchins in stripy nightshirts had gathered around the car. Alaa shouted some instruction to them, at which they all dashed forward, plucked the rocks from beneath the wheels (they were its only brakes!) and with a graunch of gears and a cloud of smoke, Alaa urged the car into motion.

At first our Egyptian driver seemed content to potter along at 20 mph, and we started to relax as we pulled slowly away from the banks of the Nile along a strip of tarmac amid a sea of sand and rocks. But soon he spotted a tour bus ahead, and Alaa promptly hunched forward over the steering wheel and gunned the car's tired old engine in order to get alongside the bus as it entered a blind bend.

As the bus gained speed around the long curve, Alaa raced alongside it, finally drawing level with the front of the bus as the road straightened out. To our immense relief there was nothing coming the other way, as it was a good half a mile before our car had gained enough advantage over the accelerating bus to pull back to our own side of the road in front of it. At which point Alaa relaxed, sat back in his seat and slowed back down to 20 mph again.

I looked nervously over my shoulder as the coach loomed up behind us, but at that precise moment Alaa took a right turn towards some huge stone monuments, so we never discovered whether the bus driver was furious and intent on running us off the road, or whether Alaa's driving was normal in these parts.

Over the next few days we discovered that Alaa was one of Luxor's more considerate and predictable drivers, and his car more roadworthy than most. He became a great friend and guide, patiently waiting while we explored some of the most amazing temples and tombs in the world, and he even took us to meet his wife and children and have lunch at his home. A wonderful experience, if a little nerve-wracking at times, and one we would not have missed for the world.

Back at our Oradea apartment, we had just enough time for a bite to eat before John from the EveryChild office called for us. A tram-ride across town took us to Oradea's 'English Club' where we were to be guest speakers for the evening, at John's invitation.

Here we met a dozen men and women, all yearning to speak better English, and told them of our travels. After we'd explained our motorcycling mission to Eastern Europe and our earlier 11,000 kilometre bush ride around New Zealand, we were bombarded with questions. These were mostly about European politics! It was a subject we were unprepared for. In the run-up to Romania's accession to the European Union, many wanted to know about EU membership and were clearly desperate to gain European support for their backward economy.

"Is Tony Blair trying to break up the EU?" asked one. As usual, the media has a lot to answer for.

Walking back across town later – no tram tickets were available – we were stopped in our tracks by the ornate and beautiful Vulturul Negru (Black Eagle) hotel and shopping complex which stood out from the bland, utilitarian buildings that surrounded it. We were impressed with this example of architectural excellence and hoped that Romania's EU membership would permit more artistic endeavour to replace the gloomy communist cityscape.

The last quarter-mile of our evening stroll was enlivened by a sudden downpour, so we dodged from cover to shelter, arriving dripping and breathless for an unnerving ride in the antiquated lift, as a thunderstorm threatened to knock out the power and leave us stranded halfway to the seventh floor. The lights flickered and the lift lurched and groaned more than usual, but eventually it delivered us to our flat where sleep seemed even less likely than usual.

In addition to the storm's cracks, rumbles and flashes, we had a rave party thumping away at the rear of the building and the usual cacophony of trams, traffic and the constant clatter of the textile factory at the front. It was far too hot and humid to close the windows and Viv had a real job finding any sleep, while I did my usual trick of snoring the night away.

7

Vlad And The Hazards Of Romania

Day 10, Saturday July 2nd, Oradea

It was still pouring next morning as we packed up and set off at 6.30am, walking in our riding gear to retrieve our bikes from the 'safe parking' compound a mile away. Viv had a great idea – we should also wear our crash helmets for the rain-lashed stroll across Oradea in order to keep our hair and the insides of our helmets dry. It worked, but we got some funny looks from the early city-goers who probably thought we were Martians.

We were pleased to see our bikes again, despite the downpour, as we'd felt uncomfortable with them locked away out of sight for so long – plenty of time to be stolen – but they were fine. We splashed carefully over the cobbles and through the puddles back to the apartment and started the laborious job of ferrying our luggage down from the 7th floor – me doing multiple journeys in the groaning, smelly lift, while Viv stood guard over the bikes.

By 7.15 we had everything clipped, locked and strapped on the Hondas and I was just updating my dry-wipe route board when Ady and her husband Michael arrived. They wanted to take photos of us for EveryChild and the press (we had not warranted a press photographer the day before) but we made an uninspiring sight, bedraggled and dripping in the early morning gloom and rain.

I handed over the flat keys and a million Lei to Ady, a contribution to the water and gas we'd consumed, plus a minor donation to their limited funds. By 7.30 we were on

Looking cheerful, despite pouring rain, we prepare to leave Oradea, Romania

Viv (left) and Bob set off from Oradea in the gloom, unaware of the horrors ahead

the road to Cluj Napoca, riding carefully in heavy rain along the Crişul Repede valley, heading further east.

The road here was not too bad at first, but the other road users caused us constant concern in the tricky conditions. They were either dead slow in ancient, wheezing vehicles followed by clouds of choking smoke, or even slower horses and carts, or stupidly fast 'flash gits' in Mafia-money Mercedes, tearing through tiny hamlets without a care or thought for others.

After dodging the additional hazards of rush-hour city Cluj Napoca, we headed south, first to the amusingly named Turda and then on a minor road along the Mureş Valley to Alba Lulia and Sebeş, right through the heart of Transylvania. However dodgy we thought the roads were, we had it easy compared to the locals living here between 1456-1462 when Vlad III, Prince of Wallachia, more commonly known as Vlad the Impaler or Dracula (son of the dragon), ruled with such brutality that a legend was born.

Bram Stoker's fictional vampire called Dracula was tame compared to the real thing who put to death somewhere between 40,000 and 100,000 men, women and children by the most gruesome methods imaginable, and then some. We tried not to think about this grisly past and concentrate instead on the present dangers we faced as we headed deeper into the forests and mountains of central Romania.

At Sebeş we found a cafe and took a break from the rigours of the road over coffee and sandwiches. The last couple of miles had been much more taxing, with a plethora of hazards to add to the wet riding conditions. Here are just a few of them:

1) Tyre grooves: On Romania's tired, beaten-up old roads, the heavy lorries lean towards the verge due to the camber of the road and their overloaded chassis. The result is a tyre groove near the centreline of the road and a much deeper one near the road edge, where the combination of tyre-trench and displaced tarmac sometimes creates a ridge over half a metre high.

These ruts and ridges can destabilise a motorbike massively and in places it is impossible to ride out of them. On one occasion, Viv got stranded while trying to change lanes at traffic lights, when the vehicles in front of us came to a standstill following a minor bump. She wanted to go around the obstruction, but could not get her bike up out of the rut she was in, over the ridge and into the next lane!

2) Potholes: Not your normal dinner plate-sized hole in the road. Oh no. These are often a metre or more across and up to half a metre deep. Fail to spot and dodge one of these in time and you can puncture tyres, break wheels, damage suspension and snap motorbike frames and luggage carriers, not to mention being pitched off your bike.

3) Slumps: These are not potholes but can be just as deadly. These are where the substructure of the road – maybe an underlying drain or culvert – has collapsed, leaving an almost invisible hollow where the road has dropped. Hit these at anything above jogging speed and the suspension bottoms then fires you out of the saddle, shortening your spine in the process.

4) Horse poo: A novel hazard that you don't see much on British roads, but with lots of horses and carts in Romania, there are frequent piles of steaming horse droppings, made even more interesting to ride over when heavy rain turns it into a slimy slurry.

5) Slick tar: Not only road repairs, but whole sections of road, especially in bends, are polished glass-smooth by vehicle tyres and lack of road maintenance. In the wet these are treacherously slippery.

6) Diesel: Romanian trucks have leaky tanks and faulty filler caps. But with their own oil wells in the south of the country, this is of no concern to the truckers who spread liberal libations of slippery diesel oil over all the roads. In the dry this is dodgy, but in the wet the combination of oil lying over a film of water is deadly, especially on bends. If you are mega-observant, you can sometimes see the faint blue tint of diesel spills and then ride as if on ice to keep your wheels underneath you.

Choosing a line through the ruts, potholes, slumps, horse poo, tar slicks and diesel spills is challenging, to say the least. The only option was to slow down and tip-toe through the worst sections, even if this meant being overtaken by the lorries we had just passed and which were, of course, being simultaneously overtaken by black Mercedes doing 100mph – preferably on a blind bend!

These are just a few of the road-surface hazards. But however demanding of your attention, you can't spend too much time looking at the road surface, because you have to keep a check on ...

7) Road signs: Those that haven't fallen over, been driven into, rusted away or shot to pieces, that is. For some reason, everyone with a gun seems to find road signs irresistible for target practice, the satisfying 'clang' of a wounded road sign must make up for the absence of hunted-out wildlife, perhaps?

If you can read a sign, trying to decipher its contents, directions and/or instructions is an art in itself. Often a 'No Entry' sign will be invisible, because they only place these on the nearside and are therefore hidden by overgrown foliage or the vehicle in front. Lettering, spelling, colours, fonts and sizes seem totally random.

Place names are never the ones on your map and road numbers are changed at will, so finding your way can be a nightmare. Most warning signs eventually come to make sense, but their positioning and logic (like, *after* the hazard!) is totally different from the UK.

8) Dogs: But you can't spend too long looking out for road signs or trying to understand the ones that do show up, or you'll hit a dog. Romania has lots of feral dogs roaming the roadsides. Some of these will run into the road to chase and bark at horses and carts – frequently jumping up and biting at the horse's ankles which does nothing to improve the horse's humour or predictability.

Dogs will also chase cyclists and any car going slowly, as well as each other. Packs of dogs running along the verge beside you, barking maniacally and threatening to throw themselves under your wheels any second, is a serious distraction from the road surface and road signage problems.

Many dogs just amble into the road out of boredom or curiosity. Often a toot of the horn will get the dog's attention and they'll amble off, but taking avoiding action and sharp braking is often called for. The poor creatures are a major hazard to themselves as well as motorcyclists. The road can be littered with canine corpses which are another feature best avoided if you want to stay on your bike.

9) Drivers: Despite all of the above, by far the greatest hazard on Romanian roads are the other road users. The 'nouveau riche' in their Mafia Mercs were the major cause of grey hairs for Viv and me. In the space of two hours we counted four accidents – still fresh and warm.

The first was a chap who had spun off on a wet bend – one of the smooth tar hazards – and had smashed his car to a pulp around a tree. Amazingly he had survived intact and was standing beside the steaming wreckage talking on his mobile phone when we passed. What's the betting he was gabbing on his phone when he crashed? Most owners of flash cars seem unable to drive them without a mobile pressed to the side of their head.

The second was a bus with the front stoved in, the driver and another man trying to pull the glass out and restart the engine, so that the poor passengers could be delivered to their destinations. None had left their seats so maybe journeys interrupted by crashes are commonplace for bus travellers in these parts. What had mangled the front of the bus was not apparent, but it looked like the back end of a lorry, judging by the damage.

The third was a major crunch between a lorry and a car, the latter having no engine or front wheels left. This one was sufficiently serious for the police to be in attendance and a sheet-covered shape on the verge looked ominously like a body.

The fourth was at traffic lights, a shunt with three vehicles involved, their drivers all shouting and arguing with each other instead of moving their vehicles so that others might pass. Fortunately we were narrow enough to squeeze past before the fists started flying.

After our lunch at Sebeş the driving, already atrocious, became much worse. On the main road to Sibiu the driving rain, streaming roads, stray dogs and certifiable drivers made staying on board and remaining alive even more uncertain. Which was a shame because after Sibiu the terrain changed as we rode ever higher through a valley of wooded slopes, past pretty, old-fashioned wooden houses, up and over the Southern Carpathian mountain range and down into Călimăneşti.

By now it was 4.30pm and after nine hours of struggling to stay out of trouble on Romania's nightmare roads, we were done for, physically and mentally. Fortunately, Călimăneşti turned out to be a picturesque little spa town and we found a small hotel with a double room which was slightly smelly but cheap enough at £14. Out of our window we could see other guests taking the curative spa waters that had been piped into the hotel's tiny outdoor pool. But as their white limbs disappeared into the thick green pea-soup water, we decided to forgo this dubious pleasure and took long, hot showers instead.

We later discovered that the wonderful spa waters here are used to treat chronic digestive diseases, liver and gall bladder disorders, and diseases of the renal and urinary system amongst many others. Call us wimps if you will, but we counted ourselves lucky that we stuck to the showers in our room.

Somewhat restored, we walked to the grand old 'Hotel Central' standing majestic and proud in its leafy grounds, with steep roofs and spires, balconies and verandas inviting us in with a gothic charm. We succumbed and were shown into a vast dining room for supper alongside hundreds of OAPs. After the torments of the day, we probably looked no different from the white-haired wrinklies spilling their soup into their laps at the next table.

Whether the waiter thought we were part of the pensioner party, or there was only a fixed menu, we never quite deduced, but he promptly presented us with a meal of roast chicken and cheese-encrusted chips, cabbage salad and bread rolls, followed by cherry pancake puddings. Together with a couple of bottles of the local beer and a peach juice for Viv this little lot came to £4.50. If you are looking for a bargain basement holiday, we can recommend the pensioner package to Călimăneşti.

Hotel Central provided fine pensioner dinners in Călimăneşti, Romania

8

The Road To Hell

Day 11, Sunday July 3rd, Călimăneşti

We slept well, but both awoke with headaches, probably a result of the intense concentration and focusing on the road hazards the day before. But there was no time to dally as we had promised ourselves to get out of Romania that day, come hell or high water. Little did we know we were about to experience both...

More squally rain and violent gusts met us as we rode out of pretty little Călimăneşti on roads awash with water and mudslides. Here the roads are steep, narrow and twisting as they descend from the Carpathian highlands to the vast plain of the Danube valley below. We hadn't been rolling twenty minutes when we came across the first fatal crash of the day.

The dangers of the steep hairpin bends were obvious to us, especially with rivers of rainwater streaming down the broken and patched surface. And no driver could have missed the mammoth yellow signs spelling out 'Dangerous Bend' in English as well as Romanian. Yet on the third such bend a lorry was upside down beyond the parapet, its cab crushed flat, while four chaps stood around in the relentless rain, waiting for emergency services to arrive. There was nothing we could do to help, so we wobbled on down the spiralling, broken road, picking our way between the rivers, rocks and potholes, being overtaken by trucks whose drivers appeared oblivious of the risks.

Down in the valley we rode into Râmnicu Vâlcea, a big, bustling town full of even more impatient motorists, some of them actually nudging my bike with their bumpers to make me get out of their way. They succeeded. One thing you can't do on a motorbike is play dodgems with cars and expect to win. With my panniers bearing battle scars, we gingerly made our way out of town in increasingly severe weather conditions. The wind and rain had now increased to biblical proportions, so gusty we were constantly cuffed by great fists of wind that threatened to knock us off our bikes.

Through the driving rain and our streaming visors we could make out further Romanian road safety features. These took the form of wrecked cars, mangled almost beyond recognition, set up on stands beside the road as a grisly warning to passing motorists, who sped past us unheeding. We gripped our handlebars, gritted our teeth, and pressed on into the tempest, determined to get out of this nightmare alive.

As we approached Piteşti's oil and gas fields, bright flames spewing horizontally from their pylons, sheets of rain drenched us and even stronger gusts slammed into us from ahead, almost bringing us to a standstill and mocking our puny efforts to escape from this crazy country.

After Piteşti we were cheered to find ourselves on the broad A1 motorway, but even here the road surface switched from good to abysmal with no warning. We soon learned to scan ahead and slow to 20 mph when we saw the surface colour or texture change – the only clue to another hideous patch of broken surface which made our bikes buck and bounce violently.

The manic motorway finally brought us closer to the capital, Bucharest, and our eyes were peeled for signs to the southern ring road, clearly marked on our map, to avoid getting tangled up in the city's traffic. But there were no signs, no alternative route, and we were sucked into the city via a long, awful one-way nightmare of potholes, trenches and floods.

Rain was hammering down and the wind was blowing pedestrians' brollies inside out and the wild conditions seemed to make the city drivers more demonic than ever. The last thing we wanted was to be wrestling our heavily-laden bikes through the manic traffic of the capital and we searched desperately for any sign of a road that might lead us south for Ruse and the border with Bulgaria. But it seemed there was no choice but to go through the city centre and soon we had two new factors to contend with: road works and tramlines.

The road works were horrifying – huge trenches, some of them deep enough to swallow us without trace, but without any bollards or fences, just yawning chasms in the road, abandoned by workers in the worsening weather. Of course, most of these were full or rapidly filling with swirling brown storm waters, so where the road ahead was awash there was no telling if there was a road surface beneath, or a death-trap waiting for us. We had no choice but to follow the vehicles ahead and see whether they drove through the flood waters or disappeared into a trench.

Chris Rea sang about the Road To Hell, but I bet he never experienced anything as terrifying as our ride into Bucharest that day. As we were sucked ever-deeper into the whirling vortex of the city-centre traffic, we came across the next challenge – tramlines. These were not the flush-with-the-road-surface tramlines you might find in Sheffield. Oh no. These were fully-raised train rails like steel barriers, criss-crossing the road at oblique angles. The cars in front of us lurched, bumped and banged their way over these rails, slithering sideways as their tyres scrabbled for grip on the wet steel.

"My God," I whimpered under my breath, *"they can't mean us to ride over those, surely?"*

But with a honking stream of impatient traffic behind us, we had no choice. We couldn't stop. We couldn't take a different route. We had to try to ride over them. I turned my bike to approach the rails as near to right angles as possible, stood up on the footrests and blipped the throttle as I pulled up on the handlebars. On a lightweight trials bike, this technique would lift the front wheel sufficiently to clamber over the rails, but on a fully loaded touring machine the chances of success were slim.

By some miracle my front wheel bounced over, and with a crash and a squirm, my rear wheel followed. Another bump, crash and squirm and I was over the second rail. And then I remembered poor Viv behind me – how on earth would she get over them? A glance in rain-spattered mirrors and I saw her standing up, willing her top-heavy 650 over the rails, using the skills she learned on our New Zealand off-road epic a few years before.

But she wasn't enjoying it any more than me. I'll let her journal entry tell it in her own words...

"In Bucharest we enter a whole new ball game. Looking for signs to head out on the right road, the chaos begins. It's like a bad dream, with every bad thing you can imagine all happening at once.

"Suicide drivers barge through, trying to knock us from our bikes. Huge trams thunder along like scary monsters, sounding their horns impatiently. Decide, they say, decide now whether you live or die.

"Intersections, one after another. No order, no signs, not enough eyes to see in all directions at once. Just go, over bumps like kerbs, ramps, cobbles, polished with rain, and potholes – great caverns of water to ride through.

"People crossing, dogs dodging through the wheels. Then a funeral, now a wedding party, all the cars adorned with cloths and must stay together in procession, regardless of the traffic all around.

"Ride over the tramlines, slip and slide, bump and crash. Change lanes again and again. Still no signs. We are lost. God help us."

I was suddenly aware of something large looming up beside my left elbow. I risked a quick glance and was shocked to see it was a tram overtaking us. I looked ahead and saw the tram tracks crossing the road just in front of us. Bloody Hell! Too late to stop! The tram rang its bell in warning as I grabbed the throttle and bumped, bounced and crashed over the rails ahead of it.

Viv, even more terrified of getting left behind and lost in this city from hell, decided she would go too. With a desperate twist of the throttle she bumped, bounced and crashed over the rails just inches ahead of the tram. Miraculously, we both survived this joust with the tram by the skin of our teeth, but would we be so lucky next time?

These tramlines would be murder on a motorcycle at the best of times, but they were impossible in this screaming gale, torrential rain and with us hemmed in on all sides by honking, manic cars and taxis, all of them oblivious to the knife-edge of peril we rode, struggling to keep our big, heavy bikes upright and out from under their wheels. Another run-in with a tram and we might not be so lucky. If either of us had slipped on those rails, we'd be dead.

We had been fighting our way through this maelstrom of traffic and trams, floods and trenches, potholes and cobbles for over an hour now, and conditions were getting worse. As the rain sheeted down, almost all of the worst road hazards were invisible, hidden beneath the swirling brown flood waters. All we could do as we were forced to ride through these death-traps was hold the bars tight and grit our teeth. I'd been gritting mine for over an hour, and it didn't help.

Within the first 15 minutes of entering the Bucharest traffic, my jaw was aching and after half an hour my forearms and fists were locked in a terror spasm. Where possible I had been standing up on the footrests to try to see a way through the maze of obstacles, but after an hour of this my legs were aching and trembling from the strain. I couldn't keep this up much longer and how Viv was coping, I shuddered to think. This was utter madness. If we didn't find a way out of this hell-hole we would die, for sure. If the trams didn't get us, the taxis would.

I knew the road we needed was off to our right and, finally, after an eternity of torment, I saw a sign for Ruse. This was the border city just across the Danube in Bulgaria, the way we were headed. As we turned off the main drag my hopes soared that at last we could escape from the nightmare, but my joy didn't last long. This urban side road was even worse – full of road works, open trenches full of rainwater, and more cursed tram tracks.

Despite this I felt encouraged that we were finally on the right road, and redoubled my efforts to stay upright over the slippery cobbles, slick with mud and diesel, to lead Viv to safety.

This was a badly broken stone-block surface. Severe slumps where the underground sewers had collapsed were filled with water, like shell-holes in the Somme. In places the block-shaped cobbles had gone too, leaving gaping, vertically-sided potholes. Everything was liberally greased with spilled diesel, mud and running rivers of storm water.

The road might be awful – we were rattling and slithering over the roughest cobbles we'd ever encountered – but at least it was going in the right direction. Then my heart sank as within a mile the route was diverted around a major road closure. We were turned left and right with no signs and soon all sense of direction was gone. We had no choice but to press on in the hope of finding the way out of Bucharest.

How we didn't fall off, I still don't understand, but miraculously we stayed upright long enough to arrive at a major junction, where five roads intersected. There were no traffic controls here, just a manic free-for-all. And there were no signs to tell us which way to go either. Was there to be no escape from this madness?

Then I spotted a man standing in the shelter of a large building on the opposite side of the junction. I shouted across to Viv through the shriek of the wind, the rattle of the rain and the roar of the traffic, that I was going to try to cross the intersection, in order to speak to the man in the hope of getting directions.

Eventually we managed to manoeuvre to within hailing distance of him and I shouted, *"Ruse?"* and waved my arm at the choice of roads. I could have wept as he pointed confidently straight back down the potholed, dug-up road we had just come from.

We had been battling through this nightmare for over an hour and a half and now we had to turn around and fight our way through it all over again. I couldn't believe it. What had we done to deserve this? My arms, legs and jaw ached. I looked at Viv – her hollow, terrified eyes told me all I needed to know – I couldn't give up. We <u>had</u> to get out of this, somehow.

After another heart-stopping crossing of the five streams of motoring madness, we were back on the crumbling cobbled surface, sandwiched between tram tracks and trenches, heading back the way we came, back to the one-way diversion system around the closed road. When we got there I stopped and scrutinised the scenery through the horizontal rain for any kind of guidance. There, hidden among the roadside clutter was a tiny tin sign that said 'Giurgiu'.

What it meant, I had no idea, but like a drowning man clutching at straws, I dragged my map book out to search its fluttering pages as they soaked up the rain. Sure enough, there was Giurgiu, the last town in Romania before our crossing into Bulgaria. Hoorah!

It took another 45 minutes before we finally emerged from the death-grip of Bucharest, on to a flooded, potholed, slimy road that was pure sweet deliverance as it carried us south, away from the city.

Incredibly thankful to be alive, we pulled in to the first garage we came to, desperate for a chance to get off our bikes, drink a coffee and try to stop shaking. First we had to manoeuvre our bikes around the forecourt and down the side of the main building and out of the blast of the wind, so the storm wouldn't blow them over. Then we squelched inside to discover that there was no coffee, no nothing in fact as the storm had knocked out power supplies to the whole region.

George, one of the two garage attendants, could see we were in no fit state to carry on and fetched two broken chairs, the only two in the building, for us to sit on while we dripped and shivered and recovered from our ordeal. We were soaked through to our underwear but there was no point in struggling out of our saturated riding jackets and overtrousers. We couldn't begin to get dry here in this draughty, powerless fuel station, so we sat uncomfortably in our cold, wet clothing, wriggled our toes in our boots full of water and hoped to warm up a little as the fear subsided.

Using his long-forgotten schoolboy English, George kept us entertained by chatting about Romania and his hopes for the future. Everything would be better when they joined the European Union, all their problems would be solved, he said. George told us about his life, his family and his home, showing us on a map where he lived in Bucharest and inviting us to stay with him.

We thanked him for his generosity, but assured him that nothing would ever persuade us to ride back into that city. So then he wrote down his name and telephone number for us, saying if we ever had any kind of a problem – wherever we were – to call him and he would come and rescue us!

George was very sweet, but after half an hour of dripping mud and rainwater on to his shop floor, our arms and legs had stopped trembling and we decided we must press on and try to get out of Romania while we still had enough daylight to do so.

With the storm's gusts doing their best to blow us off our bikes, and rain rattling like bullets on our visors, we struggled south and by mid-afternoon arrived in Giurgiu, a sprawling port town beside the vast River Danube. As we entered the town, all signs for Ruse and Bulgaria vanished and we promptly got lost once again. Knowing we had to cross the river, we headed down to the docks but soon realised we had gone wrong as there was no river bridge here.

Back in Giurgiu town, and with help from a garage, we eventually found a sign saying *'Duane – Customs – Vada'* and finally got to the check point. We were through the Romanian exit side in 15 minutes, but there was a bewildering lack of directions in the vast, empty marshalling yard that followed and it was only when the span of the bridge appeared in the gaps between crumbling warehouses that we found our way to the vast 1.74 mile-long structure over the Danube.

Here, high above the wide river, looking down on ocean-going ships carrying goods up from the Black Sea, the storm had another determined attempt to blow us off course and into the rust-streaked parapet. But we had ridden through Bucharest and survived – nothing could stop us now! We bumped over the uneven surface of the 'Friendship Bridge' which was built in 1954 and remains the only road and rail crossing between Romania and Bulgaria.

On the Bulgarian side we had a 20-minute wait while our passports and vehicle documents were checked before we could get the stamps we needed and rode out of the border control, straight into another problem. The only road out of the customs point was a one-way section that dropped down between high concrete walls... and under a sea of water!

Ahead of us a car driver had stopped just short of the brown gloop which extended for a quarter of a mile and looked sure to submerge his vehicle completely. We pulled over and discussed what we should do. Snag was there was no other route out of the border control area and we couldn't spend the night there.

Just then an articulated lorry rumbled slowly past us and descended into the water at walking pace. It was time for a snap decision, and I made it. I shouted to Viv: "Let's follow the lorry. Just keep moving slowly and whatever you do, don't stop!" and set off after him.

This was madness, but after all we'd been through already that day, it seemed almost normal. I followed the lorry as its huge wheels descended deeper into the flood and soon I was standing up for better balance at this walking pace. I could feel the water washing over my boots and around my legs and told myself not to look down. Instead I bent my knees to get a glimpse of Viv in my mirrors, and there she was, right behind, standing up as her bike sank deeper into the mire – good girl!

Concentrating on the lorry ahead, I could see his wheels were now fully submerged and the water was nearly up to the container on the trailer. My God! How much deeper does this go? I could feel the steady pull of the water on my lower legs and felt sure the Varadero's spark plugs must soon go under and stop the engine. Like most modern bikes, our Hondas' exhausts exit up high near the seats, so as long as water was not ingested through the air intakes, and the spark plugs stayed dry, we might just make it.

I prayed there were no potholes or bricks hidden beneath the swirling brown waves. If we hit something and toppled over in this depth, we could easily be trapped and drown. Then I saw the lorry's wheels were gradually emerging and I felt the road, invisible beneath my wheels, begin to rise. We were going to make it! Another check in the mirrors and Viv was following faithfully, her front wheel hidden by a bow-wave of brown water.

As we emerged from the flood we pulled over to the side of the road and laughed with relief. We were amazed and exhilarated, standing beside our trusty steeds as they dripped, hissed and ticked while the water drained away.

After this the road south into Bulgaria was a joy, despite frequent rough patches, the odd pothole or two and increasingly heavy rain. We felt we'd escaped from purgatory into paradise. Between the sheets of rain we could see lovely countryside and sweeping bends enticing us onwards towards our destination.

Even the road signs were fun, as they were all in Cyrillic, so deciphering anything was tricky. We had to stop and work them out letter by letter to be sure we were heading the right way. Fortunately our experience with the Greek alphabet while holidaying in Cyprus gave us some clues and we deduced that 'Бяла' was in fact Bjala, 'Плевен' was Pleven, 'Полски Тръмбеш' was 'Polski Trambes and 'Велико Търново' was Veliko Tarnovo – our destination for the night.

We splashed onwards through the torrential afternoon. After a spectacularly rain-lashed 60 miles of Bulgarian countryside we finally reached Veliko Tarnovo, where rivers were running down the steep cobbled streets. We pulled up opposite Hotel Tseverets and I waded across the street through a fast-flowing, ankle-deep stream that was pouring down the road, and pushed open the door.

Only then did I take off my helmet, as my hair was the one remaining dry part of my body, and squelched inside. I must have looked as though I'd just swum across the Danube to get there and I quite expected the receptionist to shriek and tell me to go back outside.

Instead she flashed me a sweet smile, apologised for the weather and welcomed us to stay for as long as we liked. She provided us with an excellent room, breakfast included, for 100 Bulgarian Levs (£40) per night and after we had splashed to and fro across the river running past the door to ferry our luggage in, we finally felt we could start to relax.

Having wriggled out of our sopping clothing – our boots were full of water, gloves full and dripping, jackets saturated – we rigged up a series of washing lines in our room, perching gloves and boots over table lamps, to start the long process of drying everything out. By now it was 6.30pm and after the most arduous day's riding we'd ever encountered, we were famished. Our receptionist had been so helpful, perhaps she could suggest somewhere to eat?

"Yes. I know just the place for you, and I will call for a taxi to take you there – it's too far to walk," she replied, as she picked up the phone. Cushty!

A few minutes later we were sitting in a fabbo restaurant – all oak beams and roaring log fires, with Sting and the Police boys playing on the sound system – being served humongous pizza and delicious Bulgarian wines. It seemed a fitting reward for having survived the road through hell. We feasted royally and slept soundly, oblivious to things going bump in the night.

ROMANIA
BULGARIA
Veliko Tarnovo
Gabrovo
Stara Zagora
Haskovo
Plovdiv
GREECE

Coffee break at a biker café near Charlesville-Méziers

Gasthof Eberl in Hattenhofen near Munich

Postcard-pretty Lake Bled in Slovenia

Wooden house & bike-shed at Svigelj Sobe in Bled

Lake Balaton, Hungary, as we might have seen it…

'Lawrence of Arabia' fixing his bike after the fairing broke

Tram rattling past our apartment in Oradea

Vulturul Negru (Black Eagle) hotel in Oradea

Angry floodwaters swirl close to houses in Veliko Tarnovo

Mist rising from the swollen river Jantra, Veliko Tarnovo

The Black Sea is blue! Rocky shoreline at Sozopol

Sunny Sozopol street scene viewed from our balcony at the 'Ginny'

A common sight on Romania's roads.
Bikers need to take extra care here.

© Vereshchagin Dmitry

And if the lorries don't get you, the roads probably will! © Falk Kienas

9

Cold Comfort

Day 12, Monday July 4th, Veliko Tarnovo

We awoke to a very cold and damp room, with no sign that any of our gear had started to dry out at all. Over breakfast we found out (different receptionist, same helpful service) that the hotel had a problem. With all the rain, water was gushing up like a spring inside a cupboard just outside our room and they'd had to remove 120 buckets of water during the night to stop the place from flooding. So that explained why our room felt cold and damp!

We also discovered on the morning TV news that the previous day's atrocious weather had caused dramatic floods throughout Romania and Bulgaria, especially in the Danube valley which we had crossed yesterday. Over a dozen people had been drowned, houses and bridges had been washed away, there had been landslips and mudslides and collapsed roads. Several more people had died from lightning strikes. With a shudder we realised we could easily have been another statistic on the news bulletin.

The receptionist said we were very lucky to have got into Veliko Tarnovo at all. Shortly after we arrived the river Jantra, on whose dramatic bend this picturesque town was built, had burst its banks and all roads out of town were closed. Just as well we'd planned to stay for two nights and a much-needed day's rest and recuperation.

We kept the TV on all morning, as much for its heat and drying ability as anything, and the news pictures continued to show more floods, ruined homes and destroyed roads and bridges. The death toll rose with each successive bulletin as news reports filtered in from remote villages. We felt someone must have been looking after us throughout that torturous and traumatic day.

As the storm slackened to fitful, gusty showers we stuffed our sodden boots with newspapers and rearranged our soggy clothing over the TV and lamps in an attempt to dry them, but it seemed an impossible task in the cold, damp room. By midday the weather had improved sufficiently for us to venture out, so we took a walk around town and marvelled

Steep cobbled street in Veliko Tarnovo: pretty, despite the rain

Looking up the Jantra valley from Veliko Tarnovo, Bulgaria

at its stunning views over the tree-clad, horseshoe-shaped river surging brown and deadly below. With only treetops poking through the chocolate brown, roiling flood waters, some of the lower houses looked to be in imminent danger of being swept away.

Higher up, where our hotel and the main shopping streets were located, there was no such danger and we were able to appreciate the steep, winding alleys, flights of stone steps, terracotta pantiles and quaint little shops. In one of them we found a two-pin plug to replace the faulty adaptor for our kettle. In the windows of several others were charming, detached, four-bedroom country houses in acre-plus gardens for sale at £6000! But we resisted the temptation and bought an umbrella instead, which was more suited to our immediate needs.

By mid-afternoon there were enough gaps in the showers for me to check over the bikes and lube the chains, in the hope that we might be able to leave next day. The road south to 'Стара Загора' (Stara Zagora) and 'Хасково' (Haskovo) – our next rendezvous with the EveryChild programme – remained closed, but our cheery receptionist (number one again) reckoned there was a chance it might be reopened next day.

Lastly I contacted the EveryChild office in Sophia, the Bulgarian capital, and spoke to Rada, who said the charity's local team in Haskovo were looking forward to seeing us, if we could get there. The road conditions looked doubtful, she said, and she was concerned about our safety on our motorcycles, having heard of many cars being washed off the roads, or hit by falling rocks and trees.

Gulp. Oh well, nothing more we could do but see what the morning would bring... except to fortify ourselves for the morrow with another of those stonking mega-pizzas.

Day 13, Tuesday July 5th, Veliko Tarnovo

At breakfast next morning our helpful receptionist (number two) called the road-info helpline and reported that the road out of Veliko Tarnovo to the south was now open – hurrah! – but was only passable with great care. Much as we liked this pretty town and were nervous of what we would have to deal with en-route, we needed to press on. The charity had lined up a big press reception for us on the following day and, since raising EveryChild's profile via maximum media coverage was our primary mission, we didn't want to keep them waiting.

By 9am we were rolling again, this time in bright sunshine under blue skies. The roads, however, were not so encouraging. The floods had left piles of sand and gravel in the road, plus deep puddles and occasional mini-rivers coursing across the tarmac. Thank goodness for our off-road riding experience in Cyprus and New Zealand. We were frequently standing up on the footrests, wrestling our bikes – Ewan and Charley style – through rivers of mud and water.

The road wound its way up the Jantra Valley and, rounding a bend, abruptly disappeared into the black hole of an unlit tunnel. From brilliant sunshine we were plunged into pitch black darkness in an instant. No warning signs, no lights, no nothing. Fortunately we were only doing around 50mph and as fear gripped my heart I spotted the dim glimmer of light from the far end of the tunnel, hidden around a corner. All I could do was to head for the light, hoping not to hit the invisible tunnel sides or a kerb on the way, as Viv followed my rear light doggedly.

A few seconds later we emerged blinking into brilliant sunshine again and pulled over at the roadside to gather our wits.

"My God! That was like the Black Hole of Calcutta," said Viv. *"It's a good job we always ride with our lights on. If I hadn't had your rear lamp to follow, I'd have ridden smack into the tunnel wall!"*

How many drivers had done just that, we wondered? It served to remind us that nothing can be taken for granted on these Eastern European roads and we needed to be prepared for anything. Fortunately, after our fright in the 'tunnel of doom', the road continued more predictably, twisting through forests to 'Габрово' (Gabrovo) and over a high pass before dropping down to 'Казанлък' (Kazanlak). Here we stopped for coffee and fuel and found we needed to show our passports before using our credit card, which seemed a reasonable precaution in a land where crime has largely filled the gap left by communism.

After 'Стара Загора' (Stara Zagora) we passed through lovely countryside, the fields full of people toiling away at their crops and the road full of horses and carts clopping and rattling along. We were getting better at deciphering the road signs and by lunchtime we'd passed through 'Димитровград' (Dimitrovgrad), crossed the raging Marica River unscathed, despite parts of the road being missing where the floods had scoured them away, and ridden into the large town of 'Хасково' (Haskovo).

Compared to some of the hilltop villages, Haskovo looked smart and prosperous and had the feel of a thriving regional town. With help from drivers we located Hotel Haskovo, recommended by Rada, and got ourselves checked in. As in Oradea, there was no safe parking for our motorbikes, so we called Gergana Chukova, EveryChild's Haskovo Project Assistant, for advice. She turned up a few minutes later speaking excellent English and said she could arrange parking for the bikes.

We followed her car on a trek around town and by 4pm and two parking lots later, we had the bikes parked, locked (remembered them this time) and covered. We had brought a couple of thin, cottony motorcycle covers to hide the bikes from prying eyes and this open, town-centre parking lot seemed the ideal place to try them out.

In a discussion with Gergana we decided to leave the bikes here while we went on project visits in Haskovo, 'Пловдив' (Plovdiv) and 'София' (Sophia) over the next three days. But by the time Gergana has deposited us back at our hotel, we were on to Plan B. After all the hassle and stress of Bucharest we felt we could do without a visit to another capital city and decided to cut out the Sophia visit.

That sorted, we took an evening stroll around the attractive, pedestrianised town centre and found a cafe for supper. Despite the Cyrillic menu and zero spoken English we managed to order food that was both recognisable and edible, which we considered a triumph of luck over language.

Day 14, Wednesday July 6th, Haskovo

By morning we were on to Plan C: we would take our bikes with us to Plovdiv after all. It would be too much hassle to split our luggage in two, leaving all our riding gear, topbox and panniers in Haskovo while we took an overnight bag to Plovdiv – we were bound to leave behind something we needed. And besides, we didn't feel comfortable leaving our bikes so exposed and vulnerable in Haskovo town centre while we were miles away in Plovdiv. It was pure paranoia, of course, but our Hondas were not only our transport, they were our trusted friends on this voyage into foreign lands and the risk of having them stolen was just too unsettling to contemplate.

We tried to explain all this to Gergana and her male colleague, Marian, when we met at their office first thing, but I'm not sure our reasons made any sense to them. If they were annoyed at our dithering and plan changing, they were much too polite to say so and accepted our new itinerary with grace before telling us all about their work in Bulgaria.

As in Romania, EveryChild's main thrust here is working with others to bring about important changes in children's lives. Thanks to a recent change in government legislation, disabled children are now allowed to go to mainstream schools and kindergartens, a vast improvement on the very poor special schools that catered for them previously. These were so bad, many parents kept their kids at home where they received no education at all.

Within six months of the new ruling, the Haskovo EveryChild project had been set up to facilitate the inclusion of these disabled children in regular schools. Working with the Haskovo municipality, the Ministry of Labour and Social Policy, the state agency for child protection, the parents of disabled children and, of course, the schools and kindergartens themselves, EveryChild quickly got things moving.

First up was providing accessibility – ramps for wheelchairs, adapted toilets, elevators etc to enable the 55 school-age disabled children to use the schools and kindergartens. Next was educating the parents on the benefits of mainstream school education, otherwise they can refuse to send their children. And last, but not least, recruiting and training resource teachers for the kids' special needs.

In their first year 21 disabled children graduated in Haskovo and the town now features the greatest number of included children in the whole country. Now the plan is to replicate these good results across the rest of Bulgaria. At the time of our visit, only ten other locations in the country had any kind of inclusive education in mainstream schools for disabled children.

The project is funded primarily by sponsorship of the children by folk in the UK. EveryChild's most valuable fund-raising comes from caring people committing to a small monthly payment on behalf of their sponsored child. These monies, along with other donations, then go to fund all the excellent work that EveryChild undertake, achieving amazing value for money, as we had seen in Malawi.

At the time of our visit, just 14 of the children had sponsors and 35 more were hoping for kindly UK citizens to take up their cases. Having sponsored children in Malawi, Bulgaria and St Petersberg, we can vouch for the system's integrity and the sterling work that is achieved with such minimal funding. If you'd like to know more, go to: www.everychild. org.uk or contact them at EveryChild, 4 Bath Place, Rivington Street, London EC2A 3DR. Telephone 020 7749 2468.

Fully briefed on their work, we set off with Gergana and Marian for one of the kindergartens, where the press were waiting for us. As we rolled up in the car, the eight pressmen and women – from four different newspapers, two radio and two TV stations, including Bulgarian State National TV – were all poised, cameras clicking, flashbulbs popping and cameras rolling.

Then there was a major altercation between the media people and the EveryChild staff. The press had been expecting the triumphal arrival on motorcycles of this intrepid duo, who'd just ridden all the way from the UK, and instead we turned up in a car! They were understandably riled and not at all impressed that our bikes were in a secure car park elsewhere in town.

Gergana and Marian were really getting it in the neck, and although we couldn't understand what was being said, we gathered they were being harangued big-time. Realising the press needed photos and footage of us on our bikes, I suggested we could go with them to the parking lot after the interviews were over and then we could ride our bikes for the required pics.

That calmed things down and we were then grilled by the press who wanted to know why we'd come to Bulgaria, what we thought of the charity's work on behalf of these children etc – Gergana doing a cracking job of translating for us. Once we'd been thoroughly interrogated (it was quite unsettling having microphones shoved in our faces), we had a few minutes for me to have a whistle-stop inspection of the kindergarten while Viv grabbed a few precious moments playing in the sand pit with our own sponsored child and his classmates.

Then it was a quick dash to our hotel to get into our leathers, boots, helmets and jackets, followed by a zoom to the parking lot to meet the press again. After a few laps riding around the town square to simulate our arrival while the cameramen did their stuff, our ordeal with the press was finally over. We rode back to our hotel to pack up, pay for our room and load up the bikes for the ride to Plovdiv, 50 miles to the west.

After all the hassle and panic, heat and pressure in Haskovo, it was good to be back on our trusty bikes and out on the road again. We soon covered the distance up the Maritsa Valley, through lush arable farmland on moderately good roads and arrived in the sizeable city of Plovdiv at 3pm. That was the easy part. Finding our hotel was another matter.

We had hoped to stay somewhere quiet on the outskirts, as our experience of riding in cities so far had been traumatic. But there were no hotels there, only in the centre, we'd been told by Gergana, who'd kindly booked us into the centrally-located Hotel Leipzig for two nights.

At first this seemed a doddle. There were even signs for the Hotel Leipzig as we rode into town, but then these evaporated just when we needed them and we had no clue where the hotel might be. So we pulled over beside a large building to ask a pedestrian.

"Hotel Leipzig, molya? (please?)" I asked, waving a piece of paper with the name on, as if that might conjure up the place out of thin air.

The young chap I'd accosted looked baffled, which was not too surprising, given my atrocious pronunciation.

"Hotel Leipzig?" he queried, in disbelief.

"Da, da, Hotel Leipzig," I confirmed.

He shook his head in wonder, turned on his heel and pointed upwards. There, in metre-high illuminated letters over the third floor balconies it read...

'Хотел Лайпциг'

"*Hotel Leipzig!*" he said, with a smile, to these simpletons from another planet. Well… would you have recognised it?

We rode our bikes on to the pavement, just around the corner from the hotel entrance, to unload them, and were immediately approached by a tall and handsome young man who turned out to be the parking attendant. Not only that, but he had a bike of his own – a Kawasaki 1100, he told us – and his name was Bob!

He would be honoured, he said, to look after our machines for us personally over the next few days and for the first time in a week we felt reasonably reassured our bikes would be safe. That didn't stop us double-locking them and hiding them under their shroud-like covers, mind you...

Our room on the ninth floor – another series of arduous marathons up and down in a wheezing old lift with the luggage – was slightly skanky, but cheap at 70 Levs (£27.50) including the parking service. And it afforded great views over the city from a massive – and deadly – window. UK Health and Safety would be apoplectic if they saw these windows. One turn of the handle and the huge metal casement window swung <u>outwards</u> on side hinges, like a door, opening from ceiling to knee level, and taking you with it if you weren't careful. Sneeze here and you'd be a goner!

Outside there was no balcony, no ledge or even a windowsill, just a vertical drop nine floors to the pavement below. How many Leipzig guests had beaten the old lift to the ground floor in this way we could only speculate.

Since the window was our room's only ventilation and the day was hot, heavy and humid, we had no choice but to keep it open and we thanked God that we were not here with small children. What a nightmare that must be. As it was, we tended to hold on to each other when we took a look at the view, not quite trusting ourselves to avoid falling.

After washing our smalls and ourselves in the shower, we set off for a stroll around Plovdiv, which turned out to be a pleasant place with tree-lined boulevards. And the Bulgarians also proved to be lovely people in every respect but one: they had no concept of pavement courtesy.

If we came across someone waiting for a bus, or chatting to a friend, it did not occur to them to step aside to make way for us to pass. We had to walk right up to them, nose-to-nose, and say: *"Molya? (please?)"* while waving an arm in the direction we wished to go. And even then they looked puzzled, with furrowed brows, before realisation finally hit them: *"pedestrians... want to pass by... I have to move!"* and then they shuffled to one side to let us pass.

Stepping off the pavement to go around them was not an option as the vehicular traffic in Plovdiv slowed for no-one, not even on pedestrian crossings, and roared past the kerbs oblivious of those on foot. So it was all the more puzzling that the locals didn't make way for fellow pedestrians. Had this happened once, we would have dismissed it, but at least a dozen times on the short evening stroll we had to stop and ask people to move themselves so we could walk by – it was really weird.

Crumbling masonry falls from first floor balcony
in Plovdiv, Bulgaria

Before we could conduct further socio-behavioural experiments with the good folk of Plovdiv, the heavens opened and we dashed back to our hotel, where we slept fitfully with the rumble of traffic and distant thunder coming in through the open window, and the prospect of one of us stumbling out of it in the night a disturbing possibility.

My record with windows and night-time wanderings is not good. As a young boy I suffered from frequent nightmares and sleep-walking, and as the youngest of six children this behaviour kept my siblings and parents on their toes. So that the household might get some respite from my midnight gibbering and crashing about, I was banished to the far end of our old house, a former bakery, where a separate set of stairs led to my bedroom above the kitchen. It was not at all unusual for me to wake up downstairs in the pantry, where I consoled myself with one of Mum's mince pies.

But not all of my nocturnal perambulations were so fortuitous. On one occasion my sister Mary was woken by my cries of *"Kee-kee, Kee-kee!"* – my childhood nickname for my friend, Keith Kilby.

As she rubbed the sleep from her eyes, Mary spotted me sitting astride the lowered sash window of her first floor bedroom, leaning out and calling my pal's name. She just managed to drag me in before I toppled to my doom. After which, all doors were locked to prevent me from sleep-walking to disaster. And it was with this thought in mind that I finally drifted off in Plovdiv beside the open ninth floor window of death, with Viv instructed to grab me if I so much as twitched in the night.

ROMANIA

BULGARIA

Karnobat

Stara Zagora

Nova Zagora

Burgas

Sozopol

Plovdiv

GREECE

10

Distant Bombs

Day 15, Thursday July 7th, Plovdiv –
'Хотел Лайпциг'

Not surprisingly, perhaps, we didn't feel all that chirpy
when we stumbled out of bed in the morning. In addition to
a night of fitful sleep, filled with dreams of falling from high
buildings, I discovered I had picked up a stomach bug and
diarrhoea, while Viv felt unwell and nauseous too.

At least we didn't have to ride our bikes while we
had dodgy tums, as the day was scheduled for visits to
EveryChild's Plovdiv Family Support Project and, in another
part of town, their Children's House.

By 10am, when Maria – EveryChild's Plovdiv Project
Manager – called to pick us up, we had smartened ourselves
up and pulled ourselves together sufficiently to put on a show
of normality. Apart from making the toilets the first and last
facility we visited on our tour of inspections, we managed to
focus on the charity's good works.

Their Family Support Project started in 1993, initially to
provide financial support to impoverished families so that
their children's basic needs were met – things like shoes,
clothes, electricity, fuel. But after some years it became
apparent that this was only creating dependency, not self-
sufficiency. So step by step the project was changed to ensure
the families had active participation in a support system
through a range of social services.

With the central aim of helping children overcome
deprivation and grow up in a safe family environment,

EveryChild employ three social workers, a project manager and a financial manager. In conjunction with teachers, doctors, psychologists, speech therapists, advocates and mediators, the team helps prevent child abandonment and improve social inclusion. Everything from improving job opportunities for the parents to teaching parenting skills is covered, plus training in disease and drug-abuse prevention.

One example was a mother, a sole parent struggling to cope with two boys aged eleven and twelve and a fifteen year old girl. The youngest boy had a bad speech problem and was very withdrawn, with a real risk of being abandoned by his mother. After an assessment, the team helped the mother find a better job so she could support her family, gave financial assistance to repair her washing machine so she could clean their clothes and provided speech therapy for the boy. The result was a more confident and able mother, happier children and the boy responded so well to the speech therapy that he became more outgoing and is now succeeding in school.

When we called by, the Family Support Project had already benefited 300 children and looked set to help many more. But this was only one of EveryChild's activities in Plovdiv. Across town we got to see their Children's House which was just two years into its stride, catering for orphaned and abandoned children between three and twelve years old.

This home was bought, repaired and adapted by EveryChild, then donated to the municipality, which would assume full responsibility for running the place in a further six months time. In the meantime, EveryChild had established a unique facility which was being replicated elsewhere, the charity justifiably proud that their Children's House pilot-scheme had been adopted as the national standard throughout Bulgaria.

Staffed by 12 social workers, the Children's House provides, as near as possible, a family type of environment for up to 19 dumped and damaged kids at any one time. This means a loving and caring home – often the first they've ever experienced – from which to attend school and kindergarten, go on holidays, camps, walks and shopping trips. The result is that many children become re-equipped to fit into a normal family, some then returning to their own homes or being adopted or fostered.

We were very impressed with the thought and energy that had gone into this scheme and the great results it had already achieved, paving the way for a new system across the country. But by early afternoon our grumbling tums were wearing us down and we were pleased to be dropped back at the 'Хотел Лайпциг', which we now recognised as our hotel with views to die for.

I groaned in unison with the ancient lift as we inched up to the ninth floor and retired to bed as soon as we reached our room. Our gloom wasn't improved when we found CNN on the TV and heard about the London bombings that morning. Our first thoughts were for our own children, who might have been visiting the capital, but text messages soon verified they were okay.

Then we realised that EveryChild's head office was near the bomb blasts and their staff could easily have been on the commuter trains or buses caught up in the horror. A phone call established that they too had been spared and our thoughts turned to all those unknown souls who had been killed or injured that morning, and the many more who would be traumatised for years to come by such stupid, senseless violence.

It seemed an ironic contrast between EveryChild, busily exporting their compassion and care to the children of the world, and these fanatics importing their hate and mayhem to the streets of London. What will it take, we wondered, for them to see that bombs and bullets solve nothing. It is only love that conquers all.

Chapter 10

Day 16, Friday July 8th, Plovdiv

Next morning I still had the trots and felt decidedly weak and feeble, which was especially frustrating as a short holiday on the Black Sea coast was awaiting us, if only I could pull my mind and body together sufficiently to get there. It would be a 200 mile ride and I was doubtful I'd make it, but we were keen to be moving on from Plovdiv and the room with the death-plunge view.

After a reviving cup of tea, I felt well enough to take the slow route to the ground floor to wash the bugs off the bikes and check their chains and oils. The theory was, if I survived this minor mission intact, maybe we could get back on the road to see how far we could go that day. In truth, after bending and crouching around the bikes for a few minutes I felt lousy, but decided to chance the journey anyway, as we both needed a change of scenery.

After a half-hour of hot and sticky work manoeuvring all our gear – two panniers, one topbox, one rucksack, two helmets and two jackets – out of our room and into the lift, then out of the lift and on to the bikes, we were finally ready to go at 9.30am.

The gods must have taken pity on us, for in spite of a complete lack of road signs in the city, we miraculously found ourselves on the right road for 'Бургас' (Burgas). As the early morning mist gradually lifted, we discovered we were travelling through yet more fields of sunflowers, all with their faces turned down like sad children. After 'Стара Загора' (Stara Zagora) the sun had begun to break through and with this the sunflowers all cheered up and turned their faces to greet it.

We stopped to refuel and I had an amusing tug-of-war with the pump attendant girl over the filler hose. Filling a motorcycle tank brim-full, without spilling any over the paintwork or hot engine, is quite a tricky task and we don't trust anybody else to do it. This is not a problem in the UK where pump attendants died out with tigers' tails, but this young lady insisted her boss wanted her to do it and pulled the nozzle out of my hands.

So I closed my tank cap and made to ride off, saying I bet her boss would be less pleased if we spent our money at the next filling station instead. At which point she relented, handed over the nozzle and let us fill our own tanks.

The further east we travelled, the hotter it got and the more crazy the traffic became. The road to Burgas revealed a novel overtaking phenomenon, where five or six cars and trucks would <u>all</u> pull out simultaneously to overtake a column of slower moving vehicles, despite the fact that only the first one could see any oncoming traffic. When this first one pulled in at the last minute to dodge the bus bearing down on him from the other way, the remaining four or five vehicles were left stranded on the wrong side of the road and scrabbling for cover. Jeez, what madness!

We tried our best to stay well clear of this lunacy, using our bikes' instant acceleration to power away to where we could see clear tarmac ahead. The downside of this was losing the several tons of mobile steel protection between us and the idiots pulling the same overtaking stunt from the opposite direction. I almost got hit by a lunatic overtaking on a blind bend – only my bike's slimness and manoeuvrability avoided a head-on collision – and our heart rates soared for a few minutes. Fortunately my tummy troubles had abated, or there might have been an accident of another sort.

Despite these frequent scares, the Bulgarian roads were infinitely safer than those of Romania and we made good progress as the day warmed up. Shortly after midday we found ourselves in the outskirts of Burgas, major Black Sea port and resort town, where the road from the west splits to go north to the seaside fleshpots of Sunny Beach and Nesebar, and south to the fishing village of 'Созопол' (Sozopol) where we were headed. This had been recommended by the EveryChild staff as a quiet haven of genteel relaxation, a best-kept secret amongst the locals.

Before we left Burgas however, Viv's ride was brightened considerably when she got a big smile and a cheery wave from one of two passing motorcycle cops in shirtsleeves and shades, riding BMW F650 Funduros. Viv's always had a bit of a thing for policemen on motorbikes, so this recognition by one of the Bulgarian boys in blue put a twinkle in her eye for the rest of the day.

We'd only seen three other motorbikes since leaving Plovdiv – a pair of sportsbikes that careered by like loonies earlier, and a Suzuki Hayabusa – the 1300cc super-powerbike – that had slipped past us a few minutes earlier. Five miles up the road the Hayabusa had been pulled over by the cops, who probably just wanted to ooh and aah over its bulging engine and colossally-wide rear tyre.

The Bulgarian police seemed friendly enough which probably means they got paid. On our trip to Malawi, when we drove ourselves around the country to visit EveryChild's project there, we encountered a different breed of copper, motivated by poverty. Outside some of the towns in the south there were roadblocks and police vehicle checks. These were not an attempt to improve road safety, but a crude way for the police to earn some money, a common practice in several African countries.

At the first of these we were asked to show our reflective warning triangle, but as far as I knew, our ancient little Nissan hire car didn't have one. The smiling lady police officer then informed me that this was an offence and I should be taken to the police station, charged and fined. However, she said, she was thirsty, so she would let me off if I bought her a Pepsi cola from the nearby stall and she held out her hand for the money.

I was so incensed by this blatant corruption that I felt disinclined to hand over any cash on principle. I dithered and said I wasn't sure I had the money for a Pepsi, which she must have realised was a blatant lie, but I guess she wasn't keen to drag me off to the police station either. So we stood there in the road at an impasse.

Then I remembered the kind gift of vegetables from the father of our sponsored child in the north. These had been rolling around in the boot for a few days as we had no idea what to do with them. So I retrieved them from behind our suitcase and offered them to the police lady.

"Can I give these to you as a gift?" I asked her, *"For you and your family to make a meal this evening, perhaps?"*

She accepted graciously and waved us past the barrier, looking somewhat incongruous in her peaked cap and khaki uniform, holding an armload of vegetables. But that's what life's like in Africa. People make a living however they can and for some a police uniform is a means of raising on-the-spot fines to put food on the table. In eastern Europe, despite warnings of bogus police and dodgy roadblocks, we didn't encounter any problems from the law, thank goodness. Just plenty of scares from the lawless.

Smooth, sweeping bends of a super new coast road soon carried us south to Sozopol, which turned out to be a very pretty little resort built on two rocky peninsulas jutting out into the Black Sea. Far from dark and gloomy, this inland ocean looked deliciously blue and sparkly in the afternoon sunshine.

After two 'no vacancies' at hotels on our ride through, we decided on a change of tactics to avoid more laborious stop-start and turnaround manoeuvres in the heat of the day. I left Viv sipping an orange juice at a cafe, guarding my Varadero and our luggage, while I nipped down the narrow back streets on her more nimble Transalp to search for suitable accommodation. An unassuming house with the unlikely name 'Ginny' proved to be just what we were looking for. The friendly owner showed me the top floor suite featuring circular bed, separate lounge and huge bathroom with a corner bath – all rather luxurious for just 70 Levs (£27.50) per night, with the use of a garage opposite for storing the bikes securely a mere 5 Levs extra.

I booked us in for three nights then popped back to fetch Viv, who was suitably impressed with my discovery, although neither of us could quite work out which way to lie on the circular bed. Before we could flop into it for a well-earned rest, we took a turn around the town to buy a few supplies and find a cool breezy 'Ресторант' (restaurant) for a light meal (my tum was still a bit dodgy). Later, with a gentle zephyr and lots of silence coming in through the open window (no death-drops here, thank goodness) we slept roundly in our circular bed.

ROMANIA

BULGARIA

Sozopol

TURKEY

GREECE

11

Black Sea Bliss

Day 17, Saturday July 9th, Sozopol

We're on holiday, hoorah! We awoke feeling refreshed and relaxed and fully deserving of a two-day break at the seaside before tackling the long ride home. After breakfast we set off for a walk around our little peninsula, then around the larger one to the north, passing on the way a wide sandy beach already full of toasting tums and browning boobs.

Oh we did like to be beside the seaside -
Black Sea at Sozopol, Bulgaria

There were no package-holiday Brits here. Apart from the locals, it seemed Italians were the principal discoverers of this unspoiled haven and they, of course, looked elegant and suave in their designer thongs and shades, glistening with expensive sun-lotions and topped off with perfect coiffures.

Infinitely more interesting to us than the beach scene was a little museum, tucked away in the 2,500 year old fortifications, where a very helpful lady told us all about the town's history. When we commented on her perfect English, she told us she also spoke fluent French, Polish, Czech and Swedish, and could converse passably well in another half dozen languages besides. Blimey!

Sozopol had been a strategic Black Sea port ever since it was founded in 610BC by a Greek Hellenic colony. They traded wine, salt and textiles from the Greek world of Athens and Rhodes with the local Thracians who produced copper, honey, grain and wood.

The town was originally called Apollonia in honour of their god Apollo and during the 5th century BC the Greek sculptor Calamis constructed a 30 foot high bronze statue which stood in the town's temple of Apollo. Then the Romans conquered the region in 72BC and took the 13-ton statue

Traditional stone and timber fishermen's houses
in Sozopol's old town

*Sozopol harbour hosts quaint fishing boats,
a military quay and Black Sea port*

to Rome where it was put on display until it mysteriously disappeared, never to be seen again. So if you've got a rather large metal man hidden behind your garden shed, I'd whip it down to Antiques Roadshow sharpish. Might be worth a bob or two.

Under the Romans the town became Sozopolis (City of Salvation) when they converted to Christianity in the fourth century AD. Then in 812 the town was incorporated into the first Bulgarian Kingdom under Khan Krum and prospered for many centuries only to fall to the Ottomans in 1453. Over the centuries since, the Bulgarians swapped ownership with the Turks, whose Ottoman empire regularly swallowed much of the country.

All historied up, we resumed our exploration of the pretty town. This part of Sozopol, a maze of narrow cobbled streets, featured lovely traditional fishermen's cottages, with stone-built ground floors, overhung by elaborate wooden upper storeys. Many had been restored with beautifully-carved wooden beams and balconies. All the houses were topped off with red pantiles and looked charming sandwiched between the light blue sky and azure sea.

On the far side of the northern peninsula was Sozopol's sizeable harbour, enclosed by an island and adjoining sea walls. Inside were the docks of a commercial port, a small fishing harbour and a military quay lined with rows of small, rusting missile-launcher boats, a relic of the Soviet era.

By now the day was once again heating up, so we took our time over coffees in a shady harbour-side cafe, rested our legs and watched the world go by. Despite being a customer, the cafe charged Viv 30 'Stotinkies' (the small coins she had renamed 'stinkies') to use their toilet, which seemed to be a feature of all the town's cafes. We consoled ourselves with the fact that the coffees cost us about 10p.

After a leisurely afternoon snoozing back at the 'Ginny' then emailing family from a nearby cyber-cafe, we were enticed into an Italian restaurant for lasagne, macaroni and chips, accompanied by beer and fruit juice, for around £6 the pair of us. Holidays here could be just the ticket for thrifty travellers, we decided.

Our second Sozopol slumber was not quite so peaceful because the weekenders had arrived and celebrated their Saturday night with firework parties. But with the room's air-conditioning humming gently and the windows closed, we shut out the noise and slept soundly with hardly a whiz-bang to be heard.

Walking around Sozopol's main peninsula revealed charming vistas

Day 18, Sunday July 10th, Sozopol

Next day we pulled on our boots and headed off in the other direction, past a down-market district of grockle-traps. Beyond the doughnut and kebab stalls, flip-flop and inflatable toy kiosks, was another long beach already packed with sun-worshippers. There was no awareness of skin cancer here, with many nut-brown and bright red people and, more distressingly, a lot of badly-burned young children too.

Further on the crowds thinned out and we headed towards the golden sands with the idea of cooling our feet with a paddle in the sea. But as we drew closer we realised this part of the beach was frequented by nudists of the flabby variety, so beat a hasty retreat back to the road. This soon led us around building sites where lots of apartment blocks and big, posh villas were going up. Sozopol's days as a quiet and genteel resort may be numbered...

As the temperature soared we trudged back to the 'Ginny' hot and tired and in need of a rest, but after lunch and a nap were ready to tackle motorbike maintenance (me) and packing (Viv) ready for an early start on the morrow. Then we did a count up of our remaining Levs and 'stinkies' and decided we might just squeeze supper out of our remaining 14 Levs – about £5.

Amazingly, my meatballs and chips plus Viv's moussaka in a nearby cafe came to only 8.80 Levs, so we treated ourselves to pancakes and ice cream and still had enough spondulicks left to buy a nice little painting of Sozopol's fishing harbour as a reminder of our Black Sea holiday.

We figured we didn't need cash for our dash to the Romanian border the next day, since every fuel station we'd encountered so far took payment by credit card, and we already had enough bread, cheese, apples and water to make our breakfast and lunch.

We might have bought gifts for the family back home, but we had no room to carry them and anyway, we couldn't make out what most of the labels said, let alone find amusing product names. Shopping in foreign supermarkets is usually good for a laugh provided you have plenty of time on your hands and are not desperate to locate some vital medication.

In Sozopol we found nothing to match the range of wonderfully-named goods we once discovered in a Montenegro mini-supermarket, where you could buy: 'PLASMA KEKS' baby biscuits, 'BARPY' choc-nut spread, tins of 'CRAP' (it was actually carp, but someone had tragically misspelled it), 'PLACENTA' shampoo, 'BREF' toiler cleaner (one sniff took your bref away), 'ARF' kitchen cleaner, 'FLEXO GAL' plasters, 'TRONKY' chocolate bars and, our personal favourite, 'NOBLICE' biscuits. They tasted a lot better than they sounded.

ROMANIA
Giurgiu
Ruse
Razgrad
Shumen
Varna
Obzor
Nesebar
Burgas
Sozopol
BULGARIA
TURKEY
GREECE

12

Heading West Again

Day 19, Monday July 11th, Sozopol

Up at six, we were soon struggling down four flights of steep and narrow stairs (why do we always get the top-floor room?) with our luggage, helmets and coats, then retrieved our faithful Hondas from the garage opposite. An early start, we decided, would get us back across the Danube and into Romania before the day got too hot and wearisome, as it seemed to do by mid-afternoon here. Our start may have been early, but it wasn't very slick.

Whether the two-day break had dulled my navigational senses, or the early start meant we weren't fully awake, it wasn't clear, but what soon became apparent was we were lost already and we hadn't even left town! We had to ask for directions and then turn around to head the opposite way, which was frustrating. It has to be said that the odd road layouts and lack of good signs make life very difficult for British travellers here, and if you can't decipher Cyrillic, you're Буггеред!

Back up the coast road to 'Бургас' (Burgas), it took us a couple of attempts to find the main road north to 'Варна' (Varna) and once on it I decided it was time to fill up our fuel tanks. By this time we'd done 160 miles since the last fill up and 200 miles is about our limit. With no reserve tanks on these bikes, the first cough from the engine is usually the last and means you are pushing, so the next garage would have to be our refuelling stop.

This should have been no problem. Despite the often poor

119

roads, the majority of service stations in Eastern Europe – usually OMV or Lukoil chain garages – were excellent. With well-stocked stores, spotless loos and snack-bar coffee shops included, they put our UK fuel stations to shame. What's more, they all took credit cards without a hitch, making currency hassles redundant, hence our cavalier attitude with the last of our Bulgarian currency the night before.

You can almost guess what's coming next, can't you? On the main drag north from Burgas to Varna – one of the busiest roads in Bulgaria and most popular with foreign travellers – there were suddenly no Lukoils or OMVs to be seen, just scrappy little tin-pot garages with a single pump and no facilities.

We passed a couple of these expecting to find a proper fuel station in the next town, but at 170 miles on my trip counter, I decided we'd better fill up at the next garage, no matter what size or shape, rather than risk being stranded fuel-less by the roadside.

I'd no sooner made this decision when ALL fuel stations vanished! 175 miles... 180 miles... 185 miles... gulp! This was getting serious. This main coast road to Varna then became hilly and twisty, further burning up our last few precious drops of fuel. 190 miles... jeepers! We'd be walking soon. At 195 miles, with our engines sucking on fumes, we rode into a small town with a garage – hoorah!

Unfortunately it was a piddly little one and didn't take credit cards. Blast! So we had no choice but to press on, past another equally tiny garage, and suddenly we were leaving town and all hopes of fuel behind. Arggh! Then there was one last small garage and we pulled in. No, they didn't take credit cards either. They wouldn't take Euros or Sterling, or even US dollars – we'd brought some of each of these for emergencies just like this – all to no avail.

The pump attendant then said there was a bank back in town and it was our only hope for getting some useable currency. We had no choice, we had to go back. I didn't dare use up our last drop of fuel trying to find the bank, or we'd never get the bikes back to the garage, even if we had currency to pay for fuel. So we parked up outside a nearby cafe and I walked a hot and sticky mile and a half – getting funny looks as I was in black leather dungarees while everyone else was in shorts and T-shirts – to find the bank and its 'automat' to

*A fistful of Levs and 'stinkies', vital currency
in some Bulgarian fuel stations*

extract 80 Levs. I trudged back to find Viv and we blew a few of our hard-won Levs on coffee before finally returning to the garage and filling up with fuel.

Of course, within a couple of miles there were OMVs and Lukoils aplenty... Doh! But be warned, if you are ever travelling this way, there are at least 25 miles of Black Sea coast road with no fuel at all, and credit cards are not always the universal passport to freedom we may imagine.

When we got to Varna the navigational nightmare got worse. We needed to head west and inland on the A2 motorway towards 'Шумен' (Sumen) – main city in these parts – but could we find a sign for Sumen or the A2? No, we could not. After traipsing up and down various roads leading us to the docks and industrial areas, asking for directions and getting increasingly hot and bothered, we finally gave up and headed right into the city centre.

There, an old man at a bus stop pointed the way. It was not signposted for Sumen at all, despite this being the next major city just 55 miles away at the end of the motorway. No, it was signed for 'София' (Sophia). But that's the blooming capital, almost 300 miles away! All roads in Bulgaria eventually lead to the capital, or so it seems.

Finally we found a sign for A2 Sophia and thought we'd cracked it. But then the road split into two and BOTH were signed for Sophia, one in green, one in blue. We figured that motorways right across Europe are denoted by blue signs, so headed off that way... and immediately ended up down a bumpy country lane!

It was pleasant enough, slowly pogoing along between fields of yellow sunflowers, but this would take hours. All the more frustrating then that we could see the motorway, first on one side, then on the other, but there was not one single sign to tell us how to get on to it.

After 30 miles or so, we decided to take matters into our own hands and headed off down a little side track in the direction of the motorway and eventually forged a way on to it. Hurrah! But our rejoicing was short-lived as we discovered the multi-patched and giant-potholed motorway was little better than the beaten up country road we'd been on before. At 60mph we were leaping around on a pair of jackhammers and had to slow to keep our bikes and bodies in one piece.

Even bad roads must come to an end, and the atrocious A2 motorway eventually fizzled out. With no signs of any kind to inform us of anything, we had no choice but to carry on until we came to an OMV garage, where we were informed that, yes, we were indeed on the right road for 'Pyce' (Ruse), the last Bulgarian town before the bridge over the Danube.

This service station, somewhere along the road to 'Разград' (Razgrad), was a welcome respite from the rigours of the road and we were able to de-bug our helmet visors, wash our hands, make some sandwiches and enjoy a late morning picnic break. I had developed the old stress-induced, red-hot needle pain between my shoulder blades and Viv had aching knees, just 150 miles into our day's ride. Our restful days at the Sozopol seaside were already a distant memory.

Pressing on, I knew we must be getting close to Romania again when a pair of impressively long legs followed by an impossibly short skirt uncoiled themselves from the back seat of a black Mercedes as we rode through a small town looking for signs to Ruse.

I was momentarily distracted by this sudden vision of nubile naughtiness in the middle of an otherwise dreary urban landscape. My gaze scanned upward to blonde hair and scarlet lips. She can't have been more than 20 and was either a gangster's moll or a pimp's merchandise. Trouble, without a doubt.

Then the truck we'd been following turned off right without indicating. I swerved around his tailgate and resumed my search for road signs, but suddenly all the signs were blank. What's more the road had narrowed and all the traffic was heading straight at me! Something wasn't right.

Perplexed, I stopped at the kerbside and Viv pulled alongside, laughing.

"Liked her, did you?" she smiled. *"You were so busy ogling that girl's legs, you missed our turning and brought us up a one way street – the wrong way!"*

An oncoming car beeped and its driver flicked his finger to show we should be going the other direction. Curses! I knew she was trouble. I'd only glanced at the girl and ended up breaking the law. We'd have to attempt a U-turn, as soon as there was a gap in the traffic.

Viv leaned over again: *"That'll teach you to keep your eyes on the road, instead of checking out the totty,"* she laughed.

It wasn't the first time I'd gone the wrong way in a foreign country. Within five minutes of picking up a hire car in Sharm El Sheikh, Egypt, I dodged around the end of a funny plastic trestle in the road to head back to our hotel. Fifty yards later we were stopped by an angry looking policeman, who strode around to my open window and berated me in Arabic.

"I'm sorry," I shrugged. *"We're English and I don't understand what you're saying."*

His anger changed to annoyance while he thought for a minute. Finally he waved his flashing red baton at the road and said: *"This very bad for you. Egyptian man – he go calabash!"* And he thrust his hands through my window, wrists pressed together in a convincing imitation of wearing handcuffs.

"You go back!" He aimed his baton in the direction we'd just come. *"Not go past – NOT go past it!"* he said, pointing his baton at the funny plastic trestle. *"Next time – calabash!"*

I'd not been distracted by a pair of legs, or anything else vaguely worthy of my attention. I'd simply failed to recognise an Egyptian No Entry sign and almost got us thrown into jail. Not the best way to start a holiday. I made a mental note – plastic trestles in the road mean no entry in Egypt, despite them having no signs, symbols or words to suggest as much.

I prefer the Irish ones, seen at motorway slip roads around Dublin, which say, in metre-high letters: *"THE WRONG WAY"*. They always make us giggle, but only because we can read English. They would be of little use to the majority of Egyptians... or Bulgarians.

In fact the Bulgarian No Entry sign, when we'd turned around and sheepishly retraced our steps to the junction, looked very similar to the UK version, so I had no excuse for ignoring it. The Merc was still there, but fortunately the girl with the dangerous legs was nowhere to be seen, only a surly looking bloke with sunglasses and no neck lounging by the gangster car to witness our red-faced exit from town.

We finally rolled into 'Rousse', 'Pyce' or Ruse, depending which language you spoke, in the early afternoon and were processed through both the Bulgarian and Romanian borders fairly quickly after our bikes' registration documents were inspected again. Passing once more over the long, long bridge across the Danube – mercifully without the storm and tempest trying to blow us off our bikes this time – we entered into Romania and back into Giurgiu.

This was enough for one day. Although it was only 2.30pm, we'd been on the road for eight hours, covering 300 miles, much of it on difficult roads. And with all the stress of finding our way despite the lack of road signs, and keeping going despite the lack of fuel and credit card facilities, we were physically and mentally exhausted. Besides, it was now very hot and humid and we were desperate to peel off our leathers and thick jackets, helmets and heavy boots and shower away the day's sweat and grime.

However, deciding to stop and finding somewhere to stay are two very different things in this part of the world. After a tedious and sticky ride around town looking for non-existent hotels, we gave up and headed north, stopping for fuel on the outskirts of Giurgiu, at a fuel station that thankfully did take credit card payment.

I was so pleased with the ease of the card transaction that I ventured a little conversation with the cashier about the strange lack of hotels in this border and port town.

"You wanting hotels?" he asked, surprised.

"Yes, anything will do. We're tired and really need to rest," I said.

"Okay. I show!" And he came from behind the counter, placed his hand on my shoulder to turn me around and pointed at the building across the road, fifty metres further on.

"Hotel. There. See?" He laughed.

Brilliant! I would never have spotted the tiny sign that was unreadable, even this close, and would have ridden right past. Salvation was in sight at last. I thanked him and went back outside to Viv, with a spring in my step and a smile on my face.

"Follow me for a nice surprise!" I said, and rode across the street on to the hotel forecourt, much to Viv's puzzlement. It really didn't look like a hotel and the sign – 'Cosmo' – gave nothing away either.

"It's a hotel, according to the bloke in the garage," I explained, and clumped off inside to see if we could book in for the night.

I found myself in a very dark room, bumping into tables and chairs. A dining room perhaps? It was hard to see in the gloom after the searing bright sunshine outside and there was no-one about. I called out: *"Hello! Anybody home?"* Silence.

Undeterred, I walked down an even darker corridor and found a half-open door emitting a glimmer of light. This couldn't be a hotel, could it? Where was the reception desk? I knocked and shouted *"Hello!"* and the door was immediately opened by a tubby young man wearing nothing but a pair of diminutive Speedo swimming trunks.

"I... I'm sorry," I stammered. *"I was looking for the hotel."*

"Yes, okay. This hotel," he replied. *"You want room?"*

To be honest, at that precise moment, I wasn't quite sure. What on earth was I letting us in for? As I glanced nervously at his swimwear he saw my hesitation and laughed.

"Look. Is okay. Very hot, so we take swim in hotel pool. You can use it too – very good!" he said, then continued: *"My name is Cosmi. You are welcome,"* and he shook my hand wetly. *"Anything you want, you ask me – I own this place."*

He seemed a nice enough chap, now I'd recovered from the shock of his near nudity, so I booked us in and went back outside into the searing sunshine where Viv was sweltering with the bikes. She didn't seem to care what state of undress the owner was in, so long as this really was a hotel and we had a room where she could flake out.

After we'd unloaded and locked up the bikes, then dragged all our gear up three flights of stairs (yup, top floor again!) Viv hopped in the shower while I headed for the swimming pool. The thought of a nice, cooling soak was too good to pass up. But when I found it was tiny, grimy and full of jumping, splashing kids, I gave it a miss and took the shower option instead.

With ourselves and our sweaty clothes washed and rinsed, we chilled out under the ancient, rattling air conditioning unit for about 15 minutes... and then the electricity failed. I wearily pulled on some clothes and headed down to find Cosmi, who told me a fuse had blown because more than three people were using electricity at the same time!

"It's not so good, like you in United Kingdom. You have electricity all the time, no problem. Here, many problems," he said with a laugh, as he went off to some dusty cupboard to fix the fuse.

Despite his best efforts, when I got back to the room there was still no power. So we decided to take a stroll before the shops shut in the hope that time might mend the dodgy wiring circuits back at the 'Cosmo'. We couldn't quite decide whether our hotel's name was short for 'cosmopolitan' (I don't think so) or 'costs more' (definitely not), so we took to calling it 'Cosmic' in the style of Rodney from 'Only Fools And Horses', which seemed a much better fit.

Our early evening constitutional had another purpose. We'd run out of chain lube and needed to find some more. The aerosol can we brought from the UK had done sterling work keeping the chains and sprockets nicely lubricated without spreading itself all over our bikes and luggage, a function of its clever, quick-drying wax formula.

It's hard to find this stuff in the UK, so we didn't hold out much hope of finding anything similar here, where even electricity is an unreliable commodity. But our spirits were lifted when we discovered not one, but two specialist lubricant shops within 500 yards of each other. Sadly, neither had any kind of lubricant spray and so we headed back to the helpful garage opposite the 'Cosmic' where we finally turned up a can of spray-on lithium grease. This was not ideal. It would spread black, greasy filth all over the back of the bikes, flinging off the chains as they whirred round at speed, but it would have to do. Running with no chain lube would wreck the chains and sprockets in short order.

Back at our top floor luxury suite in the Cosmic (yes, I'm being sarcastic – the walls were made out of hardboard, there were no curtains and the floor lino stuck to our shoes with an unpleasant slurping sound as we walked across it) there was – amazingly – electricity! Yahoo!

We celebrated with an orgy of air conditioning and cups of tea... just as a violent thunderstorm began. At the fourth giant clap of thunder, all the lights went out once again. But looking out of the window we could see that it was not just the hotel's joke wiring to blame this time. The whole of Giurgiu was without power. Cosmic!

There was not much we could do in the approaching darkness (it's our age, you know), so we stumbled downstairs to the restaurant, where a voice in the gloom told us the kitchen was still working, thanks to gas cookers. However, it was too dark to eat in the gloomy dining room, so we'd have to sit outside, where there was still a faint glimmer as dusk hadn't fully fallen yet.

This didn't sound too promising, as the rain was now pouring down, but the waiter produced a large brolly and escorted us to a little hexagonal gazebo with a single table underneath. Here it was just about light enough for us to see each other, but too deafening to hold any kind of conversation, thanks to the rain hammering on the tin roof.

"Can we see the menu?" I shouted, foolishly, over the din. How I expected to read it, I can't imagine.

"No good for you – all Romanian," he shouted back, which saved my embarrassment.

Then he helpfully suggested: *"Chicken, chips, salad?"*

When I asked if there was anything else available, he replied: *"Yes, chicken, chips, salad for two people. Anything to drink?"*

This was like Fawlty Towers Gourmet Evening meets the Munsters. We had to laugh or we'd have cried.

A few minutes later he weaved back across the yard from the restaurant's side door, brolly at 45 degrees, two bottles under his arm, a basket of bread rolls in one hand and a candle in a jar in the other. He hadn't taken two steps before the candle blew out and I could see him mouthing Romanian obscenities but fortunately we couldn't hear a word.

He tried unsuccessfully to relight the candle with his cigarette lighter, burning his thumb in the process, until I assured him that it was okay – we could manage without the candlelit supper in the circumstances – and he stumped off through the horizontal rain once again.

By now we'd developed a full-blown fit of the giggles – everything seemed so comically absurd – and so we set to with the bread rolls.

Did I say bread rolls? Forgive the frivolity. These were cannonballs clearly destined for the modern Romanian army's artillery unit. They must have been at least a week old and quite impervious to any attack we could mount with teeth or knives. We were still banging them on the glass-topped patio table, wondering which would crack first, when I spotted our intrepid waiter weaving through the tempest with plates of food. So we stopped misbehaving, tried to stop sniggering, and awaited our next course with serious, grateful faces.

The chef may have had gas cooking, but he clearly didn't have a light to see with, or he'd never have sent out two plates of tough, inedible chicken accompanied by crisp, burnt chunks of carbon that would have been chips if they'd been rescued from the fat half an hour earlier. The salad was probably delicious but, as it had blown off the plates before the waiter reached us, it was hard to tell.

This was so bad, it was hilarious. We had a job to stop laughing for long enough to finish our beer and orange juice – at least they got these right – and declined dessert and coffee in the interests of our health.

It was now fully dark, save for the spectacular bolts of lightning which were followed scarily quickly by massive cracks of thunder. So we stumbled back up the stairs to our room with the intention of getting some sleep.

Some hopes. Besides the crashing and rumbling thunder, and the machine-gun rattling of rain on our windows, the lack of curtains (other than nets) meant every few seconds our room went from jet black to retina-searing bright light. It was like trying to sleep in an arc-welder's workshop.

And that wasn't all. Every mosquito in the district seemed to have sought refuge from the storm in our room, and we were being eaten alive, despite being slathered from head to toe in insect repellent. I couldn't stand the smell, so how did these little blighters still find me irresistible?

We were so far distant from the Land of Nod, it was a relief when the lights came back on. At least we could make a cup of tea. But our friendly garage over the road, we realised, had turned into a curse now that its huge forecourt illumination bathed our bedroom in a neon green and orange glow.

Despite all these annoyances, the trials and tribulations of the day finally won and I fell into a sleep of comatose exhaustion. Viv, unfortunately, dozed only on and off, and was hollow-eyed and fractious when I woke at 6am.

As even the casual reader will have deduced by now, I usually sleep soundly while Viv's slumber is often disturbed by noise, light or – and I find this hard to believe – my snoring. I'm usually dead to the world once the lights go out, but if I *do* get woken from a deep sleep, the results can be, well, quite unfortunate...

A few years before this ride to Bulgaria, Viv and I took a more conventional package holiday to Montenegro, that pretty, mountainous little country sandwiched between Croatia and Albania on the Adriatic coast. It had been an impulse decision based on a bargain discount offer, flying from Norwich airport, just 10 minutes from our door.

The low price probably explained why we were bussed from Split to a grim and forbidding old hotel that had no hot water and was overrun with local students. We could, perhaps, have put up with not washing for a week, but the sound of countless teenagers shouting, shrieking and running down the empty, echoing corridors was intolerable. We asked to move.

After complaining to the harassed holiday rep, who was busy relocating all the other English holidaymakers too, we were driven down the coast to Petrovac (pronounced Petrovats), a charming little seaside village. Here we were deposited in a huge hotel that had plenty of hot water and – as far as we could tell – no other guests besides ourselves. This suited us just fine. We've never been particularly gregarious, so having the run of the place and the undivided attention of dozens of bored staff was ideal.

Viv slept soundly in the deep silence and at breakfast we were endlessly amused by the waiter who wheeled our bacon and eggs across the vast, empty and silent dining hall on a trolley with a squeaky wheel. The squeak, squeak, squeak, as he set off from the distant kitchen had us in stitches and by the time he reached our table with our half-cold meals we were red-faced and spluttering and almost incapable of saying *"Hvala"* (thank you).

And then one morning we were not alone any more. A huge, dark, hulking man with no neck and a Neanderthal forehead was sitting at the next table. He responded to our cheery, *"Good morning!"* with a brief raising of his bushy black eyebrows – which revealed a pair of cold and sinister eyes – and an unfriendly grunt. He scared us both.

We decided he must be Serbian. Not because we had anything against the Serbs, but because he spoke to the waiter in a different language to the locals and the hotel was popular with Serbians, according to a leaflet at reception. And they put him in the room next to ours.

Quite why hotels which are utterly empty think it's a good idea to place their first two guests in neighbouring rooms, where they inevitably disturb and annoy each other, instead of at opposite ends of the building, is beyond me. But every time we heard his heavy boots clomping down the bare corridor and past our door, Viv and I both shivered slightly.

Once in his room, our Serbian neighbour was very quiet, except for once when we heard him shouting into the telephone in a gruff voice that must have struck fear into the person on the other end of the line. The rest of the time he was silently studying his assassin's manual or oiling his gun, according to our lurid imaginations.

That night, all was peace and serenity until 1.30am when I was startled awake from the deepest of deep sleeps by the sound of the Serbian's TV coming loudly through the wall. Not really awake but in a frenzied state of shock, I leapt out of bed, rushed out into the corridor and hammered on his door, shouting: *"Switch your bloody television off!"* at the top of my voice.

He answered, *"Molim?"* (*"Please?"*) in a muffled, groggy voice that suggested he had been fast asleep.

Then Viv stumbled out of our room and dragged me back inside before the Serbian had a chance to gather his wits and brain me. A dazed looking Viv asked me what the hell I was doing – trying to start World War Three with the only other guest in the hotel?

"*It's his bloody TV*," I said, still fuming. "*Woke me up in the middle of the night – can't you hear it?*" There was still muffled music coming from the wall.

"*That's not his TV, you idiot!*" said Viv, as she opened the wardrobe and fished around in her suitcase.

"*It's my radio – the alarm's gone off by accident and switched it on,*" she said, as she pressed a button and silenced the offending device, then took out the batteries so it couldn't happen again.

"*Oh my God! What have I done?*" I whimpered, as we crawled back into bed, pulled the sheets over our heads and waited for the disturbed Serbian to start pounding on our door.

We lay there, shaking and quivering for the rest of the night, and in the morning crept past his breakfast table, hoping he might not realise who it was that had woken him. He said nothing, but had a longer-than-normal conversation with the waiter with the squeaky trolley. When we dared return to our room we found he was being moved to the other end of the hotel, far away from mad Englishmen who rant and rave in the middle of the night.

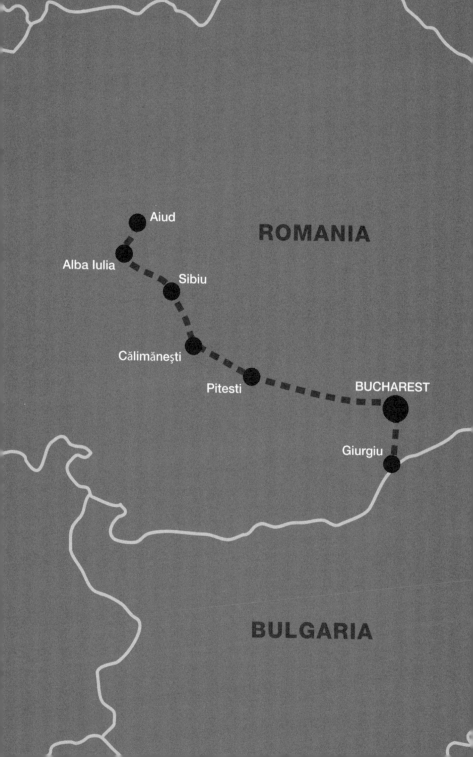

13

More Cosmic Delights

Day 20, Tuesday July 12th, Giurgiu

It was still chucking it down and rumbling with thunder as dawn feebly lightened the sky, revealing the garage forecourt under water and treetops waving wildly in the wind. This looked like a repeat of the day we had left Romania over a week previously, when floods, landslips and lightning had wreaked such havoc and we were stuck in Veliko Tarnovo with all the roads closed.

Sure enough, the early morning TV news showed reporters standing thigh-deep in floods in Piteşti – where we had planned to be at 9am that morning! It didn't take us too long to realise that we needed to stay put and enjoy the undiluted luxury of the 'Cosmic' hotel for another 24 hours, in order to let the flood waters recede.

All the river valleys were flooded to the south of the main mountain range – the Southern Carpathians – that we had to cross to get through Romania, so there was no way around the problem. And at 8am the rain was still hammering down so hard that water was pouring through a crack in the concrete end wall of our room and forming an impressive puddle on the mock-wood linoleum flooring. We consoled ourselves with the thought that this was probably the first wash the floor had received in years and maybe it would render it less sticky underfoot. In fact the water just made the lino lethally slippery instead.

We went down to breakfast, more in fear than hope, and were served a surprisingly edible omelette with cheese and cold meat, bread and jam, coffee and a huge pot of green tea. This went a long way to make up for the farcical meal of the night before and lifted our spirits considerably.

There would be no problem keeping our room for a second night, said Cosmi. We didn't bother pointing out the long list of failings. It might be leaky and lacking in curtains, but it would be infinitely better than trying to ride through a flood of biblical proportions in a storm on our motorbikes.

Half-finished and dodgy buildings provide housing for thousands in Giurgiu

*Keeping an eye on our trusty steeds at
Hotel Cosmo in Giurgiu, Romania*

*Giurgiu street scene enlivened by Dacias,
trucks and Mafia Mercedes*

We'd been there, done that and got the wet T-shirts. Our bikes were safe enough, parked directly below the balcony outside our room, where we could keep an eye on them. They were disc-locked and chained together, and besides, this weather was enough to deter all but the most masochistic of bike thieves.

By 11am it had stopped raining, so we pulled on our boots to go and check out what delights the town of Giurgiu had to offer. It certainly wasn't architecture. The rows of crumbling, grey concrete block apartments that made up most of the soviet-era town's housing looked especially forbidding with black clouds scudding over their TV aerials, and grey washing waving forlornly in the breeze.

If Giurgiu looked grim, the town's female inhabitants were adequate compensation. As the sun broke through the clouds, more and more of these slim and shapely Romanian women emerged in heels and skin-tight clothing to visit the shops, chat to their neighbours and generally show off their wares to the world. And in case you think this is just the rambling of a lecherous old man, it was Viv who first noticed this phenomenon in Oradea ten days previously, and commented on it again here in Giurgiu.

Now that she mentioned it, yes, there were lots of lovely girls to feast one's eyes on here. In a country that was one of the poorest and most backward in Europe, it seemed as if the womenfolk were determined to make the most of their natural good looks to brighten the place up a bit.

By now the midday sun was beating down fiercely and the heat and humidity sapped our strength as we legged it back to the Cosmic Hotel. Fortunately we had electricity and hence air conditioning and cups of tea to revive us, plus the means to try out our latest acquisition. Since the demise of our universal plug adaptor, we'd been unable to charge Viv's mobile phone, but in Giurgiu we found a two-pin phone charger for £2.80. This bargain purchase had just finished topping up the phone's battery when the power went off again, so we read and dozed the afternoon away until it was time to find food.

Amusing as it had been, we didn't fancy another Cosmic supper, so strolled back into town where we might have tried traditional Romanian cuisine if we could have found any. Instead we made do with what was on offer at a Stuburgers fast food joint, of which there were three on Giurgiu's main street, a food chain monopoly that Ronald McDonald would have been proud of.

Power was on when we returned to the Cosmic, which meant we could make a brew, chill out and watch the TV news and weather reports. These did not bode well for our journey in the morning. We agreed that an early night and a good sleep was our best bet for facing the roads of Romania next day, but shortly after we turned in, thinking the absence of thunder and lightning must guarantee us a good kip, a disco party started up down below. Cosmic!

I stuck a pillow over my head and finally drifted off, but Viv was kept awake until the early hours by the thumping beat and occasional shrieks and shouts of the revellers. I've rarely seen her so tired and angry, but my prayers for another power failure went unanswered and she was not a happy bunny as we packed up next morning.

Chapter 13

Day 21, Wednesday July 13th, Giurgiu

Despite our lack of sleep, we were up and off by 7am, as keen to get away from the varied delights of the Hotel Cosmic as we were to beat the traffic to Bucharest. After our nightmare experience with Romania's capital city on our way east, we were determined to avoid it at all costs on the way back west. I had taken my road atlas to Cosmi's office the previous day for some local advice on finding the missing ring road...

"Oh, yes, Bucharesti very bad. Very bad," said Cosmi. *"Last time I go, my car fall in hole and wheel broken off my car completely!*

"This is not good. Better you go ring road – but this also is difficult," he said.

"I know. Last time we couldn't find it at all," I replied, missing his point completely.

"You must look out for village called '1st December'," he said, *"Then see sign for 'ceintura'. Go this way, not into Bucharesti."*

With the unlikely-sounding village of '1st December' burned into my brain, and 'ceintura' (a belt road, perhaps?) to look out for, we headed north from Giurgiu towards the capital in trepidation. The day had dawned dull and gloomy, just like our spirits as the dreaded city drew closer. This was now our number one most-feared motorcycling destination in the world.

India has statistically the most dangerous roads, but having ridden bikes there we'd swap the deadly streets of Bucharest for the manic boulevards of Bombay any day. Dodging sacred cows ambling in the road between fleets of motor rickshaws, honking taxis, cyclists balancing impossible loads and barging buses can be disconcerting in Indian towns.

It's hard to keep your eyes everywhere and spot the unmarked, Toblerone-shaped road humps at the same time. The result is some shocking bumps and bashes that assault your spine as much as your bike's suspension. But nobody is actually out to kill you and after a few days the madness and mayhem of India's roads begin to fall into a pattern of predictably chaotic, but not psychotic, behaviour.

The only major scare we had riding hire bikes in Goa, western India, was on country roads approaching an iron ore mine, where huge dumper trucks, criminally overloaded with bright red earth, ruled the roads.

We soon learned to swerve on to the verge when these leviathans thundered into view. We even began to admire the religious slogans splashed in large letters across their windscreens. Goa being predominantly Catholic due to its Portuguese colonial past, the slogans said 'MARY MOTHER OF JESUS' and 'OUR SAVIOUR' among many others.

It was only when an ore-truck careered out of a bend we were just approaching, spilling its load as its tyres scrabbled for grip, that we thought our number was up. I just had time to shout its windscreen slogan 'JESUS CHRIST!' out loud before the driver managed to wrench the mammoth machine back from its collision course and miss us by inches.

In a country where God controls events and men are mere pawns in his plan, these holy motifs are believed to protect the drivers from death and destruction. We were grateful that someone was watching over us that day and we took to uttering that fateful slogan whenever we felt his divine intervention was called for. I hoped we wouldn't need to call on his help again this morning, as we neared the Romanian capital once again.

With eyes trained like laser-beams on every sign we passed, we eventually found the date-village... but no sign at all for 'ceintura' or anything like it. However, I did spot a tiny blue sign for Piteşti just before an overpass and decided this must be the slip road for the 'Bucharest South Circular'.

Sadly, when we got to the top of the slip road and clapped eyes on the ring road which was to rescue us from the hell of Bucharest, we were HORRIFIED!

In place of the smartly tarmacked, multi-lane motorway we had fondly imagined would transport us around the capital, there was instead a sea of mud, with gigantic, car-sized potholes full of slurry and lurching, lumbering lorries climbing in and out of the churning quagmire pits at 2 mph!

And we were supposed to ride our heavily-laden motorbikes through this?! I suddenly realised what Cosmi had meant when he said, *"this also is difficult."* Difficult! This looked bloody impossible!

Viv, close alongside me as we surveyed this vision of the Somme in winter, shouted: *"My God! We can't ride on this... can we?"*

139

"It's either this, or another trip through the centre of Bucharest,"
I shouted back. We were both silent for a minute as the
indelible vision of rail tracks and trenches, flooding and
broken cobbles, manic traffic and killer trams replayed itself
in our minds.

I made a decision and headed into the mud and mayhem
of the 'Somme' ring road and Viv, in fear of being left
stranded in Romania, swallowed hard and followed. It was
horrendous, needing all of our off-road riding skills just to
stay upright and avoid being squashed by the lorries. But
somehow we stayed on and, moving at a snail's pace, within
a mile we climbed up out of the mud and on to a one-lane
strip of crumbling tarmac.

We could have cried with relief, but there was no time
for sentimentality as there followed a long, slow grind in
heavy traffic before we could join the A1 motorway. After the
slimy morass of the first section of 'ceintura', the potholed
motorway seemed heavenly and soon the flaming towers
of the gas fields of Piteşti came into view and with it the
remains of the previous day's flooding. The roads here were
full of mud, sand and gravel, plus plenty of crashed and
abandoned vehicles on the verges.

As we climbed out of the Danube valley into the foothills
of the Southern Carpathian mountains towards Râmnicu
Vâlcea, there were frequent landslips and rockfalls on the
road. We could dodge the rocks and ride over the mudslides,
but eventually we came upon a queue of stopped traffic and
riding to the front found the road was closed.

Ahead were workmen clearing boulders the size of cars
from the road by levering them with long iron poles. And
over to our left, dangling from a rope on the rockface, was
a man with a crowbar, prising loose rocks away from the
cliff. We had a ringside seat as the abseiler swung to and fro,
sending rocks crashing to the road below. We were grateful
for his efforts when we were finally waved through and got
a close-up view of a lorry that had not been so lucky. Its cab
was completely crushed and the pulverised remains of its
cargo of tomatoes poured obscenely from the smashed trailer
as the wrecker-truck dragged it away from the scene. The
driver stood no chance.

This sobering sight was reinforced a mile further up the road
where a lorry had crashed on an uphill bend, toppling over

where the rain had washed away the road edge. Romania's dangerous roads were now more deadly than ever.

We made slow and arduous progress up the steep hills with grinding-gear lorries belching smoke in front and behind us, but gradually we ticked off the hours and the miles through Sibiu, Sebeş and Alba Lulia – the scene of yesterday's TV news reports on the devastating floods. Water still poured in angry brown rivers down the town's streets, but the nightmare torrent that we'd seen on TV, bowling cars along with it, had reduced just enough for us to pick our way through the debris with care.

By now it was late afternoon and we were exhausted from the effort of negotiating the countless hazards and horrors of the day. But all of Alba Lulia's hotels were full, we were told by the apologetic receptionist of the first we tried. So many travellers had been stranded and were stuck there in the few hotels that were not wrecked by the flood waters. This post-apocalyptic scenario forced us to ride on to Aiud, where the main street was still full of mud and gravel and all the houses bore wet stains chest-high on their walls. The locals had nowhere to sleep in their ruined homes, so there was no point in asking about accommodation here either.

Finally, as the light began to fade and with it our hopes of finding anywhere to sleep, I spotted a rough-looking truckers halt up a steep gravel drive on our left. Viv waited at the roadside with the bikes while I trudged wearily up the slope to see if they had a room.

Yes! Thank God. Somewhere to lay our weary bones. First we had to manoeuvre our heavy bikes up the gravel slope and around the back of the ramshackle building where they'd be out of sight amongst discarded engine-oil bottles, beer crates and broken glass. Salubrious it was not, but we were too knackered to be fussy and quickly got the bikes locked together and covered.

We lugged our gear up a rickety and tortuous spiral metal staircase, which was barely clinging to the outside of the building, to reach a grimy, unlit passageway and finally located our door and ventured inside. A bare light bulb illuminated a dismal room featuring a lopsided iron bedstead covered with a motley assortment of odd sofa cushions in place of a mattress.

"Jesus Christ!" said Viv, in a rare moment of religious fervour. *"Do we have to sleep on that?"*

"It's a lot better than most of the locals will be sleeping on tonight," I replied. *"And we don't have a choice. Neither of us can ride any further, can we? Let's just dump our stuff and go see if there's any chance of getting something to eat. At least we've got a roof over our heads,"* I said.

Back down the scary staircase we found a small room with tables and chairs which passed as a cafe and a tall, young mini-skirted waitress who did her best to make us feel welcome. She played British rock music for us and smiled a lot as she took our order for one of every item on the menu. This cost more than our room, but we figured comfort-eating would calm our nerves and besides, the total bill for the room, meals and drinks for both of us came to less than £20.

The waitress had a colleague who did nothing but gabble endlessly on her mobile phone to "many boyfriends" we were told, plus a plump, middle-aged woman who produced our surprisingly good meals from a kitchen out the back. Totally stonkered after our truck-food-fest and wiped out by the day's long and difficult ride, we fell asleep on our bed of many cushions by 8pm. Only to be woken at 9pm by a group of noisy guests arriving, and again at frequent intervals throughout the night as doors slammed, the staircase creaked and other odd noises disturbed our sleep.

14

The Penny Drops

Day 22, Thursday July 14th, somewhere near Aiud

By 6am a grey dawn was filtering through the thin and tattered curtains, so we gave up trying to find a comfy position on the higgledy-piggledy cushions, stared at our bloodshot eyes in the cracked mirror and shuffled off downstairs for a mug of tea and an egg-on-toast breakfast.

To our amazement, the tall, young waitress was still there, looking weary and dishevelled, but still smiling as we paid up and rode away at 7am. I blame our innocent, country upbringing for the fact that we were 200 miles away and sipping mid-morning coffee before either of us twigged that we'd just spent the night in a brothel.

As the penny finally dropped, we at last understood the makeshift mattress, the 'many boyfriends' and the waitress's sympathetic smiles as she answered the naive questions of a couple of clueless clots on motorbikes.

As it was she probably felt less knackered than we did. Viv was shivery and feeling sick, while I had a cracker of a headache and blurred vision. Not ideal for riding through a strange land where the locals had little regard for their own safety, let alone ours. Within a couple of miles we'd seen our first crash of the day. A lorry had careered off the road on a bend and rolled over. Fortunately the driver was okay and was standing nearby, smoking and looking glum while he waited for assistance.

It was hard work, that morning, coping with Romania's crappy roads, awful driving and feeling unwell too. To add to our unease, we nearly ran out of fuel again and finally resorted to filling up at a village petrol pump, where we used up the last of our Romanian Lei and hoped we could escape the country without needing any more cash.

After the manic, bullying traffic of big city Cluj Napoca we plugged on westwards via the long and arduous road towards Oradea. Before we got there our tiredness and general malaise forced a rest stop. Barely able to focus on the road ahead or concentrate on the unpredictable driving of others, I pulled in to a garage, found a piece of waste ground round the back and crashed out on the soggy grass for an hour. Meanwhile Viv, more tired but less irresponsible, dozed intermittently, while keeping one eye on our bikes and luggage.

Eventually we felt sufficiently recovered to eat the bread and cheese we'd saved from the previous evening's meal, and called it lunch. Then we dragged our weary bodies back aboard our bikes and set off again, hoping to find a way of avoiding another Romanian city centre.

Following truck diversion signs which took us around Oradea's industrial area, we skirted the worst of the city traffic and tram tracks and picked up signs for 'Vama Bors' which we prayed meant the border. It did, although the customs men there made a meal out of checking every last detail on our vehicle documents before we were finally able to say goodbye to Romania – a poor, struggling, difficult country that seemed a century behind Western Europe. We hoped joining the European Union would fulfil the country's aspirations and help it escape the odd time-warp it appeared to be stuck in.

As soon as we crossed the border into Hungary the roads, houses, cars and people all looked more prosperous – more together somehow. Within a few miles we turned off at Berettyóújfalu to follow a different, more northerly, route back to the UK. First major city was Debrecen (pronounced Deb-ret-sen) where we got magnificently lost while trying to find the road to Miskolc (pronounced Meesh-kolts) which lay to the north west, in the foothills of the Tatra mountains. I accept no blame as there was not one single sign for this, the third largest city in Hungary.

When I eventually admitted defeat and stopped (twice) to ask for directions at fuel stations, we finally got on the right road... only to find it full of road works. When I say full, I mean FULL. For mile after mile we negotiated dug up roads, deep trenches where the surface had been gouged away. And traffic lights. Lots of them. After several sets of lights, each of them red until we'd sat and waited for a workman to amble over and press a button, I started counting and over the next 25 miles we were delayed at no less than ten of the ruddy things.

It was utterly ridiculous as well as agonisingly time-consuming. It seemed as if this corner of Hungary had acquired a job lot of traffic signals and had decided to dig up the entire road network in order to justify using them all at once. They'd obviously had access to a road-grinding machine too, which had run amok across north eastern Hungary, indiscriminately tearing up the roads. However, it seemed they'd not yet managed to obtain a tarmac-laying machine. There was no reconstruction going on at all, as far as we could see, just mile after mile of endless roadworks, stretching to the distant horizon.

My map showed no alternative route, so quite what anybody was supposed to do if needing to take this route daily, it was impossible to guess. Allow an extra half a day for the journey? Or just take a few months off work, perhaps?

Back home, we all get a little impatient with the odd road work on occasion, but it's not until you've had to travel a route that is ALL roadworks, with traffic lights every two miles, for 30 miles or more, that you begin to appreciate the common sense and forward planning that operate in the UK's road maintenance system.

I was, by now, more than a little frazzled by the lack of sleep, difficult riding conditions and these absurd delays. The red-hot-needle-between-the-shoulder-blades syndrome was back with vengeance and I was definitely too tense… bordering on a marquee.

So when we stumbled into a neat and tidy little town called Polgar, not big enough to be mentioned in my Glovebox Atlas Europe, we voted with our wheels and stopped for a rest break. By the time we'd relaxed with coffees and ice creams and been welcomed by the friendly locals, we couldn't think of one good reason for riding any further.

A smart looking building calling itself 'Panzio Elephant' and with a steel mammoth on the side, turned out to be a hotel. Compared to the previous night's spit 'n' sawdust trucker's brothel, this place was palatial and the efficient male receptionist offered us a room for £23. We almost snatched his arm off.

In need of a little luxury that evening after battling our way through Romania, we treated ourselves to posh nosh in the Elephant's restaurant. It was so good, we decided this decadence was worth repeating, so booked ourselves in for a second night before retiring to a bed with a proper mattress, crisp white sheets and curtains at the windows. Sheer bliss!

"Can you see me contact lens, lad?"
Memorial statue in Polgar, Hungary

Day 23, Friday July 15th, Polgar

After a glorious night of deep, untroubled sleep, with not a sound to disturb us, we awoke rested and content. Content, but not pain-free, as we both had headaches, Viv had sore knees and I still had a spear between my shoulder blades. It would take more than one night to iron out the creases caused by the past two days' trials and tribulations.

Our first aid kit had been emptied of all painkillers during our crossing of Romania, so we set out to explore the town's quaint little shops in search of Paracetamol. This proved to be quite a challenge, as nobody in Polgar, apart from the Elephant's receptionist, spoke a single word of English. Or so it seemed.

In the tiny 'Apotek' (chemist) we asked for Paracetamol, several times, slowly and with different pronunciations... and got blank looks all round. So then we did our best to mime having a headache and were promptly offered shampoo! After a few more attempts that were worthy of RADA, if not Marcel Marceau, we were finally shown a small white box with 'PARACETAMOL' printed in bold letters on the side.

I pointed to this and said, *"Kerem?" ("please?")* to the head chemist, one of three female assistants in the tiny shop.

"PARACETAMOL" she read, clear as day.

So why, oh why, when we asked for Paracetamol and mimed taking tablets – several times – did all three fail to comprehend? My struggle to find an answer was making my temples throb even more, so I smiled sweetly, said: *"Jo, jo" ("Good – okay")* and offered a fistful of fiorints for her to help herself to. Judging by the small amount she took, our cabaret act had been worthy of a discount.

Outside, between giggles and mouthfuls of water, we both popped our 'parrots' like they were going out of fashion, then stumbled off to find somewhere to sit in the shade. This turned out to be a playground, where we sat and watched the kiddies play – fortunately you don't get arrested for this in Hungary. Yet.

As the mums loaded their toddlers on to bicycle kiddy-seats and rode away (not because their playground had been invaded by middle-aged, pill-popping voyeurs, we hoped) we realised that nearly all the wheeled traffic in Polgar was pedal-powered. What a delight, in this flat, Fen-like countryside, to see so many people using bikes instead of cars. What an environmentally-conscious population they must be...

Then a Wartburg came ring-a-ding-dinging into town followed by its trademark blue smokescreen and we beat a hasty retreat, coughing and choking, to our hotel bedroom for a lunchtime nap, reflecting that perhaps these Hungarians were just poor, rather than green.

In the afternoon we walked to the town's swimming pool, but when we got there neither of us fancied a repeat of the chemist communication fiasco with the pool staff. Viv also feared we might misread the signs and end up in the wrong changing rooms (that was the bit I was looking forward to), so we trudged back to the hotel and greased the motorbikes' chains instead. We know how to have fun!

Later another bike – a BMW GS1000 – pulled into the hotel car park and we got chatting to the Austrian couple who were planning on riding it all the way to Vladivostok – 17,000 kilometres – and back. It made our efforts look puny. Mind you, they'd only done one day so far and it was the lady's first-ever trip on a motorcycle, so only time would tell if she'd still be on the pillion seat when the bike reached the Sea of Japan.

15

Trial By Traffic Lights

Day 24, Saturday July 16th, Polgar

We were up at 5am – fully caught up with sleep by now – and on the road at 6.30 only to lose half an hour getting lost in the villages north of Polgar. Hungarian road signs are rubbish! Instead of naming the major town or city at the end of the road, they instead give only the next tiny hamlet, none of which were marked on my map.

My frustration was compounded by the continuation of the endless road works we'd been riding through ever since we crossed into Hungary two days before. Don't get me wrong, Hungary's roads desperately needed repair, but to try to do them *all at once* was sheer madness. It seemed as though all of northern Hungary's roads were being torn up, with another set of traffic lights every five minutes. Utterly chaotic.

In places where new tarmac had been laid, it was applied to one side only, while the other carriageway was a rough trench awaiting infill. We were frequently obliged to swap from one side to the other to skirt around a piece of machinery or abandoned truck, and these lane changes demanded a six-inch drop off a sheer cliff of fresh tarmac into the unfilled trench, followed by a nerve-wracking scramble back up – a serious challenge on a fully-laden touring bike.

At one of the numerous traffic light halts, Viv pushed up her visor and said she was now ready for the Evel Kneivel Grand Canyon jump. But she was laughing, so I guess the Polgar rest day had recharged her spirits. Then, just when we thought the roads couldn't get any worse we rode into a village called Csobad, which made us both smile for the next few miles.

Eventually we found our way around Miskolc and up the E71 to reach the border with Slovakia where we hoped the road mending mania would end. Before they would let us in, however, Viv was asked to remove her crash helmet. Whether these border guards couldn't believe a middle-aged British housewife would be riding a 650 Honda across Europe, or thought I was smuggling a dishy Romanian receptionist back home with me, we couldn't tell. Once they saw that Viv approximately matched her passport photo, however, they waved us through with no further comment.

As soon as we got into Slovakia the roads improved, but before we could make the most of them we needed fuel and an urgent loo stop for Viv. The first garage had their toilets out of action due to a water supply problem, so we hurriedly rode on to the next one where I filled up the tanks while Viv dashed off to find relief. A few seconds later she returned with her legs crossed, saying there was no water, and hence no loos open, here either.

Desperate by now, she spotted some bushes at the back of the service station and nipped over for an alfresco pee, only to return with a stricken look, saying there was a man behind the bushes, pruning them! If she squatted there she'd get a haircut into the bargain...

So we jumped back on our bikes and rode on to garage number three, where mercifully there was water and operational toilets. To celebrate, we both used the facilities and washed the early morning bugs off our visors. It was 8.30 and we'd already been on the road two hours.

A useful stretch of motorway got us around Prešov and then west to Poprad where we stopped at service station number four for a major bike service. Here we adjusted and lubed the drive chains, checked the oils and fluids and then scoffed our picnic lunch at 10am. That's the snag with early starts. They allow you to fit in extra meals – comfort eating to help keep the wheels turning – but these have the unfortunate consequence of making your leather trousers shrink.

From Poprad it was a short dash up the Tatry mountains to the Polish border, which we crossed without any further hassle and entered a land of wonder and mystery. This was because all the road signs, shop names, posters and notices became instantly and utterly unintelligible. In every country so far, we'd been able to make some sense of road signs and shop names – even the Cyrillic ones in Bulgaria – but here in Poland they might as well have been in Chinese.

The first town looked like an Alpine ski resort and was brimming with people and shops, but we couldn't decipher which might be a bank where we could extract some local currency and which might be a cafe, where we could spend some of it.

A pleasant-looking chap stopped to admire our bikes, so I asked him for the whereabouts of a bank. After repeating the word 'Bank' several times and finally resorting to my best Marcel Marceau impression for using an ATM, he finally babbled something in fluent gibberish, shrugged his shoulders and walked off. He probably thought I was trying to peddle drugs.

A few hundred yards further down the street I spotted an ATM and after a few attempts managed to extract some Zlotys – the local currency. First problem solved, but then we couldn't find a cafe anywhere. Most mysterious. In a town that was obviously a holiday destination and was teeming with tourists, you'd think every other shop would be a cafe, but if they were they were very heavily disguised.

On the way out of town, just as the heavens opened and fat raindrops started rattling on our helmets, we saw a shop with a large sun-shade umbrella outside and dived underneath it. This wasn't a cafe either, but was some sort of confectioners where we bought cakes and cartons of juice which we consumed while huddled under the brolly outside, waiting for the shower to pass.

When it became apparent the rain was set in for the afternoon, we dug out our overtrousers, struggled into them and set off towards Kraków. Of course, such are the joys of motorcycling, that the rain ceased and the sun shone brilliantly within five minutes and we soon had to stop to take the horrible nylon garments off again before we melted.

This gave us the chance to check out some peculiar roadside activity that had intrigued us for the past couple of miles. There were people standing beside a series of wood-and-glass cabinets on the verges and several cars had stopped so their drivers could wander from cabinet to cabinet, inspecting something within.

Utterly mystified, I walked over to investigate and discovered the cabinets were all full of smoked cheese. Small, medium-sized and large lumps of cheese, moulded into elaborate and fancy shapes and patterns and a variety of hues, were on offer. This was clearly some local delicacy brought down from the hills, so I risked a few Zlotys and bought some. We both had a nibble and, amazingly, it tasted exactly like smoked cheese! We tucked the remainder away for later and rode on.

Within five more miles it chucked it down and we got soaked. Doh! Then the rain stopped but the corrugated and polished (hah!) Polish roads became increasingly slippery and uncomfortable. By 2pm, still well short of the city, we decided we were thoroughly cheesed-off and too cream-Kraków-ed to carry on any further. We were on our third country since breakfast, after all.

So we stopped before Myślenice when we spotted a hotel of sorts. There was no mistaking the whopping great MOTEL sign in 6-foot high red letters, but Motel Czarny Lew had few other attractions. It was a square concrete construction beside a busy arterial road in an unpleasant industrial landscape. Hardly ideal, but my map showed we would soon be on the city ring road and A4 motorway to the west if we carried on, so finding accommodation could get increasingly tricky. We decided to stay here for the night and booked in for bed and breakfast.

We ended up with a very basic fourth-floor room with a loo across the corridor. It was cold and smelled of damp concrete and it took us an age to drag all our luggage up the winding flights of gloomy concrete stairs. Then we had several goes at parking, locking and covering our bikes in the rubbish-strewn car park at the rear, trying to make them look inconspicuous to the stream of traffic passing by. In the end we moved them to the front of a 24-hour cafe next door to the hotel where they would be immediately visible to all, but would be under the gaze of the cafe staff and visitors throughout the night. We hoped this would give our precious bikes their best chance of being unmolested.

A few hundred yards stroll up the busy road we came across a pizzeria where we managed to order pizzas successfully, but failed miserably when asking for a salad to accompany them. The smiling waitress instead delivered to our table a saucer of tomato puree and we didn't have the energy, or the language, to argue.

Day 25, Sunday July 17th, near Myślenice

We slept surprisingly well, despite noisy neighbours, the constant drone of traffic and my nagging worry about the bikes. After struggling down the four flights of stairs several times with our bags and kit (WHY do we always end up on the top floor?) we were well ready for breakfast by 7am. Unfortunately, we only then discovered that the motel restaurant didn't open until 8. Doh!

We didn't fancy hanging around for an hour, so went next door to the all-night cafe which had unwittingly guarded our bikes and attempted to order breakfast there. We eventually got coffee and the dry buns from hamburgers, toasted. This was a little disappointing, but since the other choices listed were 'Bigos', 'Flaczki', 'Zurek', and 'Golonka', we counted ourselves lucky.

Joining the busy, rush-hour traffic on the main drag into Kraków, we were pleased to pick up the surprisingly good motorway to Katowice. Sadly, this soon fizzled out, leaving us floundering in a town called Gliwice, not knowing which way to go. It could have been worse, we could have been lost a few miles further on in a town called Krapkowice...

My map showed a nice blue double-stripe of motorway heading north-west, past Wroclaw and reaching most of the way to the German border. But right where we were a 30-mile section of it was shown as dotted lines, meaning it was just a figment of someone's imagination. In fact, almost all of Poland's motorways were depicted as dotted blue lines on my map, so there was an awful lot of wishful thinking going on here.

On our third lap of Gliwice, still hunting for road signs to Wroclaw, we spotted a grocer-cum-bakers shop and decided to console ourselves with some nibbles for later on. Inside the shop was a long glass counter, behind which were dozens of varieties of biscuits – all of them loose.

This seemed a strange idea compared to our pre-packaged biccies back home, but it had the advantage that you could choose the exact amount you wanted. Having bought a predictably immoderate quantity, I returned to show Viv, who was waiting with the bikes. If she was less than impressed with a half-kilo of plain biscuits jumbled together in a thin plastic bag, she kept her thoughts to herself and tucked them away in her topbox.

The shop keeper had pointed the way to Opole, en-route for Wroclaw, so we set off in that direction and immediately found ourselves on a badly broken concrete road which required us to stand up on the footrests while our bikes bumped and crashed over the lumps, blocks and holes.

Within a few miles this led us on to a nice new stretch of motorway and we were just beginning to relax and settle down as we sped along the smooth tarmac when it ended in multiple road works. It seemed that southern Poland had adopted northern Hungary's philosophy of 'why tear up one road, when you can rip up all of them at once?'

The A4 motorway, which my map showed as the only longish stretch of completed dual carriageway in the whole country, had obviously been built many, many years before and had received zero maintenance since then. Now, flush with EU money, no doubt, they were making up for the decades of neglect by digging it all up.

This meant the road was reduced to a single carriageway, interrupted by frequent sets of traffic lights, alongside a massive trench where they were going right down to the soil to start again. We could understand why. The remaining concrete-surfaced carriageway that we were expected to ride on was so badly worn out it was like driving over an elongated horizontal staircase.

We assumed, naively, that this absurdly corrugated road would continue for just a few hundred yards before we rejoined the nice new tarmac once again. But as we bumped and bashed and crashed along, sandwiched in a stream of cars and trucks, the nightmare motorway continued for mile after mile after mile. Our spines were hammered – we could only stand up for so long before our legs gave out – our teeth were loosened and our vision blurred. How on earth the bikes would survive this horrendous treatment, I didn't dare think.

If we wanted to head west and get out of Poland there was no alternative, it seemed, so we plugged on, rarely able to top 20 mph, for hour after agonising hour. The only respite was when traffic lights mercifully halted our progress. As we sat in the choking queues of exhaust fumes, we were too exhausted to attempt any conversation, so we simply stared at each other in hollow-eyed disbelief.

This Polish version of motorway madness continued for an incredible, desperate, bone-jarring, unbelievable 150 miles. We kept thinking that it must surely end soon, but as the long hours of miserable morning stretched interminably into the aching hours of afternoon, there seemed no end in sight. I was convinced that any minute one of our bikes would break – a frame would crack, suspension collapse or a wheel would shatter under the constant battering. I almost looked forward to an enforced cessation of the torment. But, amazingly, our bullet-proof Hondas held together and it was us that fell apart instead, developing aches and pains in every part of our bodies.

Just when I thought that one of us must surely fall off due to exhaustion, the road finally turned to tarmac as we crossed the border into eastern Germany and it instantly became immaculate autobahn. Gloriously smooth, billiard-table-tarmac felt like heaven after the road from hell we'd ridden that day, but we were too tired to continue. We turned off into Cottbus where we found the luxurious Ahorn Hotel and slumped into its opulent comfort with heartfelt gratitude.

I was just lugging the last of our bags in through our bedroom door when Viv let out a shriek.

"Oh my God!" she exclaimed, *"whatever's happened?"*

She had just opened her topbox for the first time since we left Gliwice, to find that a flour-bomb had exploded inside. At least, that's what it looked like. We soon realised what it was. The bagful of loose biscuits had been reduced to a fine powder by the endless hammering the bikes had endured that day and finally the bag had split, allowing the mess to infiltrate everything inside. The fine dust had impregnated my wallet so completely, I had to clean every single note and coin before they would be considered legal tender again. Even Viv's teddy bear was so thoroughly coated he needed a vigorous brushing and was right off biscuits for the rest of the journey.

To avoid ruining the plush and spotless hotel room, we spent the next half hour on hands and knees in the shower cubicle, removing and de-contaminating everything, item-by-item. It was a ludicrously painstaking job as no piece of biscuit remained larger than a small crumb and mostly it resembled talcum powder. Finally, the remains of half a kilo of biscuits were sluiced down the drain and Viv made me promise to make her topbox a biscuit-free zone in future. Finally we got to soak our aching bodies and try to recover from the trauma of the day's extraordinary roads.

Eventually we recovered sufficiently to take a walk around the town, admire its elegant architecture and discover a place to eat. It seemed faintly absurd to be dining in a Greek restaurant in eastern Germany, just across the border from Poland, but we didn't let that stop us enjoying a sumptuous banquet that restored our good humour. We slept well, but I had lurid dreams of riding my bike down the escalators of the London Underground, then along the train tracks, crashing endlessly over the sleepers down pitch black tunnels.

16

Mysterious Monday

Day 26, Monday July 18th, Cottbus

The Ahorn put on a fabulous buffet breakfast, but we were still too full from our Big Fat Greek Dinner of the night before to do justice to it. We consoled ourselves by smuggling a few bread rolls out of the dining room for a picnic on the road later in the day.

After a fingertip inspection of both bikes for fractures thankfully revealed none, we got underway at 8am. More silky-smooth motorway whisked us northward around Berlin and then northwest for Hamburg. In places the motorway was under repair, but despite very narrow lanes which had cars almost touching door handles, the locals drove these sections at 80mph, no doubt muttering Teutonic blasphemies about the frustratingly slow speeds they'd been reduced to.

We made such rapid progress that we easily reached our planned overnight destination by lunchtime, so we pressed on, past Hamburg towards Bremen. Turning off the autobahn we explored the little town of Zeven for likely resting places, but finding none that took our fancy, we continued and soon became gloriously lost in the countryside. This didn't bother us too much, as we were ahead of schedule and were hoping to find another village guesthouse like the superb Gasthof Eberl in Hattenhofen which we'd enjoyed so much down in Bavaria.

But something was wrong. Despite finding several attractive looking places, they were all shut up and deserted. After riding away from the fourth such establishment, I was starting to despair. Why was everywhere shut? Was there a national gasthof strike or was there some public holiday that we knew nothing about?

Finally we entered a small town and pulled up at a smart looking gasthof, which again looked deserted apart from two chaps sitting chatting at a table outside. After I'd stood rattling the locked door and cursing for a while, one of these men came over and asked what I wanted.

Exasperated, I said, *"haben sie ein Doppelzimmer, bitte?"* – my only bit of rehearsed German.

To which he replied, *"yes, of course!"* in perfect English.

"But," I said, puzzled, *"it's all locked up – as are all the gasthofs in Germany!"*

"Yes," he said, *"of course – it is Monday! Everywhere is shut on Monday!"*

I was simply too flabbergasted (or is that flabbergasthof-ed?) to ask why this should be so. Why an otherwise orderly and sensible country should insist that all its residents sleep in their own beds, and all foreigners should not sleep at all, on one day of every week. It was simply too absurd to bear thinking about.

"Er... so, is there any way we can stay here tonight?" I asked, a hint of desperation creeping into my voice.

"Yes. Of course! It is no problem. I am the owner," he said, as he produced a bunch of keys and unlocked the front door.

We were shown to a large and comfortable en-suite room, ours for £40 including breakfast, and he gave us a front door key as well as a room key, to let ourselves in and out of the hotel, as we were clearly the only guests.

This was just way too weird to figure out. Why would an advanced and civilised country be shut on a Monday? Or was it some local custom, peculiar to North West Germany? We didn't know, but what we were sure about was we were very hungry, as we'd had nothing but a couple of small rolls since failing to eat a proper breakfast that morning. If everywhere was shut, would we find anything to eat at all?

After we had showered and changed into 'civvies', we set out to investigate. We were so pleased to find a little 'Diskont' store open nearby, we bought various items of pre-packaged snack food and sat in a park to eat them. Afterwards we walked around the rest of the town and discovered there were five takeaways, one grill and two cafes open, all full of very satisfied looking customers. Doh!

I put on my best Homer Simpson whinge: *"Why do they get all the nice yummy food, while I only got a greasy sausage roll and a bag of crisps?"*

But then Viv reminded me of my previous night's gargantuan 'Zeus Platte' which had consisted of souvlaki, gyros, pork cutlets, rice, chips and veg. She patted my tummy and reassured me I wouldn't die from malnutrition overnight. Fair enoughski.

With little more entertainment to be had in the town, which had made such an impression on us that neither of us can remember its name, we trudged back to our gasthof for an early night. I had foolishly suggested 7am when the owner asked what time we wanted breakfast. Since we were the only ones there, the kitchen staff would have to come in specially. Later I remembered I had promised to adjust and lubricate our motorbikes' chains before breakfast, so it would be an early start.

Day 27, Tuesday 19th July,
a little town somewhere near Bremen

My early morning appointment with the chains – always my least favourite and the messiest job on the Hondas – was deeply unsatisfying, as my Varadero's chain had suddenly become clapped out and impossible to adjust correctly.

What happens with these modern, high-tech motorcycle chains is that they perform faultlessly for tens of thousands of miles, requiring little or no adjustment provided they are lubricated regularly. Then, all of a sudden, they stretch in one short section which causes the chain to go slack-taut-slack as it turns, creating vibration and putting undue stress on various components, the gearbox in particular.

I'd noticed an increasingly worrying shuddering from the back of my bike the previous day and now I knew the reason why. And I couldn't blame it on the dealer service some 4000-odd miles earlier. It was undoubtedly the day-long thrashing on that hideous Polish motorway that had snatched at the chain once too often.

My best attempts at a compromise adjustment together with copious greasing would probably not be enough to get my bike home with its drive chain intact. But the chances of getting it fixed seemed remote. It was vital that the chain together with both the gearbox and rear wheel sprockets were replaced simultaneously, otherwise one part-worn component would soon wreck the new ones. Finding a Honda Varadero chain-and-sprockets set and getting them fitted promptly would be tricky back home, let alone here. UK motorbike shops rarely keep these items in stock, so it's a case of waiting while the parts are ordered and delivered. Then there's usually a further week's delay before the workshop can fit you in to get the job done.

The gasthof breakfast, by comparison, was a delight. We felt guilty that the kitchen staff had been asked to come to work specially for us and resolved to show our gratitude by consuming as many of the huge variety of cheeses, meats, breads and preserves as we could manage.

We finally got going about 8.30 on a cool, breezy morning with spots of rain spattering our visors and making the roads greasy. Back on the autobahn my bike felt horrible, with the lumpy chain causing constant vibration. Despite the usual high speed traffic on the motorway, I didn't dare go above 60mph and used the throttle gingerly, scared that the chain might come apart if it was put under too much strain.

South of Bremen it became increasingly windy and we rode through a brief but heavy rain shower. The intensity of the downpour and the ferocity of the gale soon pushed the water past flaps, zips and cuffs and I felt that familiar, unpleasant cold trickle making its way unerringly down into my underpants.

Thirty years previously I thought I had the answer to wet riding conditions and non-waterproof waterproofs. Ever since I'd given up on my faithful Belstaff Black Prince suit – a rubberised dispatch rider's garment of gargantuan proportions which kept out the rain but looked hideous – I'd been regularly soaked through. My job on Motor Cycle News and later on Motorcycle Mechanics required me to test-ride motorbikes in all weathers, every month of the year. And I was getting fed up with wet shirts, wet trousers and especially wet pants.

So when another staff riding marathon was planned for December – a three-day trip around the rain-lashed north of England on mopeds – I came up with a cunning plan. I rummaged through the countless one-piece oversuits that had been sent in as samples for testing and which lay in a jumbled heap in the corner of the office. In the mid-1970s it was all the rage for motorcycle manufacturers to produce ranges of biker clothing, mostly in yellow, green and beige nylon – ghastly, even then.

These Andy Pandy suits all leaked. Their seams were hopeless, their zips were barely covered by flaps and the rain poured through. They even made you wet on dry days as they had all the ventilation properties of a plastic bag, trapping and condensing perspiration on the inside.

But in the absence of anything better, my scheme was to go for the layered look and wear lots of suits. I'd read somewhere that multiple layers trapped air in to keep you warm and I was convinced that several suits would defeat the rain and keep me dry as we spent hour after tedious hour droning around northern England at 30mph on blessed mopeds.

As I waddled out to join the others on the bikes that first day, I was proud of the fact that persistence and lots of wriggling had finally succeeded in shoehorning me into a total of seven suits. So I was disappointed when, instead of applause, all I got from my colleagues was ribald laughter, cheap jokes and endless abuse. So what if I looked like Michelin Man? I would be dry and warm when they all got soaked and I would have the last laugh before the trip was over.

Unfortunately I had not allowed for the laws of physics or the simple facts of life. At the first fuel stop I rustled off to the loos and took so long rummaging around inside the endless layers of nylon trying to perform a simple call of nature, that all the others had cleared off by the time I got back outside. And when I finally caught them up, somewhere in the wilds of Yorkshire, it was with completely numb arms and legs. The bunched layers had effectively cut off my circulation at shoulders and elbows, knees and groin.

By the end of that first day I was down to just two suits and was as cold and wet as my workmates. Another great idea bit the dust. What was worse was the photo that appeared in the next issue of Motorcycle Mechanics captioned 'Roly-poly Bob Goddard tries seven riding suits to beat the rain... and fails!'

Modern riding gear is much better, but none of it is capable of keeping you completely dry when riding all day in a deluge, as we had in Romania. Or when hit by a sudden downpour propelled by storm-force winds, as we were in Western Germany. The rain soon stopped, but as we swapped a south-going autobahn for a westerly one near Osnabrück, the wind increased to hurricane force from dead ahead and Viv thought her arms would pull out of their sockets.

With increased slipstream buffeting from the trucks and heavy gusts causing our bikes to lurch and swerve drunkenly, we had no choice but to slow down further. It was a real battle maintaining 50mph while the articulated lorries blasted past us and their wash knocked us all over the road. It was exhausting just fighting to stay upright and pointing in the right direction.

We battled on into The Netherlands, cursing the screaming wind that was blowing unhindered across the flat lands, straight out of the North Sea. By the time we got to Arnhem Viv was complaining of numb arms and aching knees from the strain and we both needed a rest. What's more my rapidly-deteriorating chain was causing me grave concern, so I suggested we try to find a motorcycle dealer.

A helpful fuel station chap gave me excellent directions in perfect English, to a business park where we found a Honda main dealer. This place was so well stocked with shiny new bikes, as well as cars, that we didn't mind hanging about, ogling the machines, while we waited for the couple in front of us to finish being served. This was taking a long time because the chap was rebuilding a 1978 Honda Bol D'Or 900 and spares for these are as rare as hen's teeth.

His partner, Anneloes, twigged that we were Brits and in perfect English yet again, asked if we needed any help. When I explained our predicament – en-route from the Black Sea to the UK with a chain in the final stages of collapse – she quickly established that the shop not only had a Varadero chain and sprocket set in stock (amazing!) but they could fit it immediately (brilliant!).

While the workshop was getting stuck in to my bike, Anneloes then got busy on her phone, trying to find us somewhere to stay. This would be tricky, she said, as there was a four-day walking event going on and everywhere was booked up. Eventually she found us the very last room at the Parkzicht Hotel, which was a short walk from the town centre, the Karenmarkt district full of restaurants and cafes. What's more, it had private parking for our bikes and free internet access, so we'd be able to catch up with our family too. Perfect! Anneloes, you're a sweetheart, thanks.

To celebrate getting my bike fixed – a huge weight off my mind – we had a slap up meal at a great Italian restaurant in the Karenmarkt. With my worries over and a delicious pasta and Chianti supper under my belt, I slept like a baby. Viv, poor girl, spent most of the night listening to the nearby railway and road traffic.

Day 28, Wednesday July 20th, Arnhem

Before we could leave Arnhem, we had to return to the Honda shop, as they'd been unable to take payment from my credit card the previous day, due to a fault at the Visa computer centre, they said. Trustingly, they had let us ride away with a promise to return next morning to make the payment. I wonder how many bike shops in the UK would have done that for us, let alone for a couple of foreigners who were just passing through town?

But the card still wouldn't work, despite being no trouble when paying our hotel bill, so the problem was with their electronic card reader, it seemed. In the end they let us pay them in Sterling, as we had too few Euros and it was a long drag back into town to raid an ATM. All in all, the Arnhem Honda shop had provided us with a first class service. Maybe we would nip across the North Sea next time we needed work on our Hondas...

By 10am we were on our way out of Arnhem and right on cue the previous day's storm reappeared with a vengeance. Gale force winds brought violent showers hurling handfuls of rain-bullets at us and made the motorway journey past Eindhoven, Antwerp, Gent, Ostend and finally into Dunkerque a day of gruelling riding. Wrestling our big bikes in these vicious crosswinds, being slammed and buffeted by the wake of lorries, made our journey through the last three countries – The Netherlands, Belgium and France – no joy ride.

By the time we'd parked up at a Dunkerque 'Formule 1' motel, we were both looking haggard and wasted and were well ready for a reviving cup of tea, courtesy of our trusty travel kettle. Like most budget continental hotels, this one had no tea or coffee-making facilities in the rooms. They want you to spend your money buying drinks in their restaurant instead. However, this stingy truckers' stop had gone one step further and had fitted special electric sockets with weird double-pronged projections to prevent guests plugging in their own equipment.

I was incensed at this mean-spirited attitude and slumped on the bed in exasperation.

"Sacré bleu!" – I'd remembered some schoolboy French – *"All I want is a bloody cup of tea! You'd think we were planning*

to fill our panniers up with their precious French electricity and smuggle it back home."

"Hang on a mo..." I'd just noticed the bedside lamp was wonky and repaired with insulating tape. *"Maybe there's another way..."*

"Don't you come running to me if you electrocute yourself," said Viv, as I unwound the tape and pulled the lamp apart. *"What are you planning to do?"*

"Make a cuppa," I said, brandishing the bare wires from within the lamp. *"Somebody's obviously done this before – that's why the lamp is broken."*

Within a minute I'd wedged the bare wires into our kettle plug's innards, switched on the lamp and – hey presto – the kettle began to boil.

"Eh, voila!" I said in triumph. *"Ze dastardly Anglaise foil ze cunning French plan once again!"*

That tea tasted twice as good as usual and in the morning, just before we left, I re-connected the wires, re-inserted the lamp top, re-wrapped the tape and nobody will ever know.

Chapter 16

Day 29, Thursday July 21st, Dunkerque

Our last day passed in a blur. I vaguely recollect clipping on the panniers and topbox for the last time and then we wearily hoisted ourselves aboard our faithful bikes. We were ushered into a train within minutes of arriving at the French Eurostar station but shortly after the doors closed, alarms sounded and we were evacuated to a forward carriage by worried-looking rail staff.

Coming so soon after the London bombings we thought there must be a nutter with a wired-up rucksack on board and kept looking over our shoulders anxiously. But within a few minutes we were told it was smoke from a car in one of the rear carriages that had triggered the alarm. Fortunately it was smoke without fire and we were soon allowed back to our bikes while the train began its descent below the murky brown waters of the English Channel. The rest of the tunnel journey was smooth and efficient and the train ride gave us just enough time to assess the effects of a month on the road.

Viv, we would soon discover, had lost half a stone and looked slimmer than ever. But she'd had no fat to lose, so her muscles and strength were diminished. Another week of riding and she would struggle to hoist her bike off its side-stand.

I, on the other hand, had gained a few pounds and looked as though I'd eaten my way through twelve countries, which I felt was a little unfair. Less surprisingly, we both had lots more grey hair and looked as if we'd aged several years.

We pulled on our helmets for the last time and rode out of the Eurostar carriage into a typically dull and gloomy British summer morning. Reminding ourselves to ride on the left after a month of riding on the right, we had a wet and windy M25 and M11 to negotiate and then suddenly we were stuck in a lunchtime traffic jam in the middle of Norwich. It seemed both familiar and intensely strange at the same time. No tramlines or trenches, no broken cobbles or mud-filled potholes. It was great to be back!

After 4,800 miles, twelve countries, sixteen border crossings and more scares than we care to remember, we were home again. Viv dropped her bug-splattered riding jacket on the kitchen floor and said:

"It was fun. But if Ewan McGregor calls, can you tell him he'll have to do his next ride without me."

EveryChild
Helping children worldwide

ChildWorld

Issue 7 · Spring 2005

A real home and a real family

Paul Dimmick reports from Moldova on how the love and kindness of two foster parents changed a child's life forever

MAKEPOVERTYHISTORY

Why We Did It

Our big trip 'Beyond Bucharest' was inspired by Ewan McGregor and Charley Boorman, and by the excellent work undertaken by UK charity EveryChild on behalf of needy children in many countries around the world.

Having seen their work in Malawi previously, and in Romania and Bulgaria on this journey, we can confirm that EveryChild create major improvements in the quality of life and prospects for these under-privileged kids. From our research and inspections there appears to be not one penny wasted, so donors can be reassured their cash is being put to good use.

EveryChild raise most of their funds from sponsors of children in their project regions, and from donations. If you'd like to know more about sponsoring a child or making a donation, go to: **www.everychild.org.uk** or contact them at:

EveryChild,
4 Bath Place,
Rivington Street,
London EC2A 3DR
Telephone 020 7749 2468

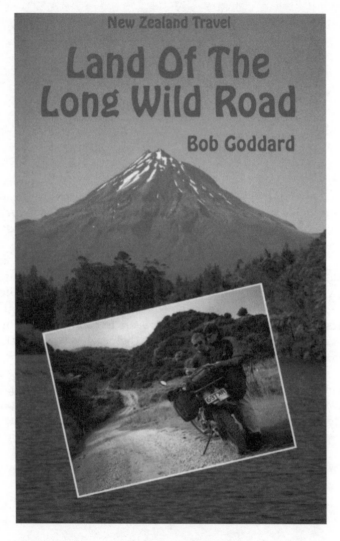

Author: Bob Goddard, ISBN: 1898030375, price: £9.95
Softback 259 pages, Colour and B&W photos and maps.

If you enjoyed Beyond Bucharest, you will love Land Of The Long Wild Road - an off-beat, observant and humorous journey around New Zealand.

Bob & Viv Goddard ride two small off-road motorcycles on gravel tracks, drovers' routes and four-wheel-drive trails into the wilderness of this fabulous and unspoiled country. With hilarious encounters and manic mishaps, they survive three-months and 11,000 kilometres of frequent soakings and occasional roastings as they battle with the elements.

Lured onward by the landscape's awesome beauty and wide open spaces their journey through rain forests and desert trails, up volcanoes and across river-beds proves to be a life-changing experience. In remote outposts, sheep stations and towns, they meet larger than life characters who offer old-fashioned friendship, wonderful hospitality and endless entertainment.

Full of vivid flashbacks and improbable bodge-ups, their humorous take on life, New Zealand, motorcycling and the art of marital maintenance, this tale is as much a voyage of discovery of themselves as the land down under. Hop on board for the ride of your life.

Whether you are thinking of visiting New Zealand, planning a motorcycle trip, or just enjoy travel from the comfort of your armchair, Land Of The Long Wild Road will grab you by the seat of the pants and put a smile on your face.

How to get your copy:

You can either visit our website and order online (www.timbuktu-publishing.co.uk), or send a cheque to: Timbuktu Publishing, Stables Bungalow, Mill Reach, Buxton, Norwich, NR10 5EJ.

Don't forget to include your full name & address and the appropriate payment (see below) and indicate whether this order is for 'Beyond Bucharest' or 'Land Of The Long Wild Road'.

Price £10 per book including P&P to UK

Price £12 per book including P&P to Europe

Price £14 per book including P&P to Rest of World

Book Reviews
Land Of The Long Wild Road

"For anyone who likes travel books and books that take a light hearted look at life, this is a great book. Bob manages to capture the beauty of the New Zealand wilderness, its history and the warmth and culture of the people; a great combination to leave you feeling good about the world.

"In addition to this, Bob's writing varies from beautifully crafted to outright comical, taking the reader on a journey through both the New Zealand dirt tracks as well as some of the farcical mishaps of Bob's youth. I really enjoyed it. It left me feeling good. I laughed out loud at least once a chapter and I wondered at the immense New Zealand scenery, wildlife and history. What more can you ask from a book? I'm looking forward to reading Bob's next masterpiece."

Richard Blackburn, Energi-Tech

"Want to ride through New Zealand but aren't quite sure how to go about it? This book is as close as you'll get to the real thing without actually going there. Over three months and 11,000 kilometres, a husband and wife team explores breathtaking New Zealand scenery and glimpses of Kiwi life aboard twin Yamaha Serows. An entertaining, well-written read. By Bob Goddard. Softcover, 6" x 9", 278pp, b/w (& colour) illus."

Aerostitch Rider Wearhouse

"I so enjoyed 'Land of the long wild road'. I read it when I was in New Zealand last Christmas so I knew some of the places. Knowing Bob and Viv made it all the more enjoyable, in fact when I was reading it, it was almost like having them in the room with me telling their tales. A fun read full of humour and real honesty."

Karen De Salis, M&K Associates.

*"**What's it about?** Grandparents and inveterate travellers Bob and Viv Goddard covered 11,000 kilometres of New Zealand's tracks and trails on off-road motorcycles. They met larger-than-life characters who offered them friendship and boundless hospitality; they braved the elements, and marvelled at the country's awesome landscape.*

"This is a vivid account of a once-in-a-lifetime journey and you have to admire the Goddards for their enterprise and grit. There are lots of photographs and line maps to show where the couple ventured in the North and South Islands – on roads that were, all too often, long and wild.

*"**Did you enjoy it?** Yes! It revived some happy memories of my own time in New Zealand.*

*"**Would you recommend it?** It's a must for anyone who's been to New Zealand or dreams of going."*

Yours Autumn Special, 2004.

Bob & Viv Goddard

Bob Goddard was for 20 years a journalist and editor with EMAP, IPC, Southern Newspapers and other publishing companies.

Working mainly in magazine publishing, Bob wrote for, edited and published titles such as: Motor Cycle News, Amateur Winemaker, Motorcycle Mechanics, Tennis, Southern Life etc.

Since 1992 he has run his own marketing and distribution business and he is also a yacht broker.

Viv Goddard, Bob's wife since 1972, has run pre-school playgroups and worked in child day-care nurseries, but most of her energy has been reserved for bringing up her own family.

Viv first rode a motorcycle in 1998 and soon became addicted. Following a succession of smaller bikes and training, Viv took possession of a 650cc Honda Transalp, the bike she rode 'Beyond Bucharest'.

In recent years Bob and Viv have travelled widely, usually exploring far from the tourist trail on motorbikes to experience the colour, culture and humour that are often overlooked.

These off-beat travels have included: Cuba, Turkey, Cyprus, Egypt, Montenegro and New Zealand, the latter being the subject of 'Land Of The Long Wild Road', their first book. For this book, 'Beyond Bucharest', they rode from the UK to the Black Sea and back again.

Bob and Viv have three grown up children and two grandchildren. They live in rural Norfolk, England.

UK

Norwich

LONDON

Dover

NETHERLANDS

Hengelo

Arnhem

Eindhoven

Ostend
Calais
Dunkerque
Gent
Antwerp

BELGIUM

St Omer

Bethune

Arras

Cambrai

Charleville-Mézières

Bremen

Zeven

Hamburg

Osnabrück

BERLIN

Cottbus

GERMANY

FRANCE

Saint-Avold
Sarralbe

Saverne

Strasbourg

Karlsruhe

SWITZERLAND

Haltenhofen

Fürstenfeldbruck

Munich

AUST

Kitzbuhel

Schwaz

Matrei

Lienz

Spittal

Bled

Kranj

SLO

ITALY

SPAIN